WORK SHIFT

How to survive and thrive in the workplace of the future

Sue Read

PIATKUS

© 1999 Sue Read

First published in 1999 by
Judy Piatkus (Publishers) Ltd
5 Windmill Street
London W1P 1HF

The moral rights of the author have been asserted
A catalogue record for this book is available from the British Library

ISBN 0-7499-1907-8

Text design by Paul Saunders

Typeset by Action Publishing Technology, Gloucester
Printed and bound in Great Britain by
Biddles Ltd, Guildford & King's Lynn

Contents

For Rothwell

Introduction

It is already clear that the traditional relationship between employer and employee is changing very quickly. As the twenty-first century approaches research shows that employers are moving away from permanent employment towards flexi-time, part-time work and job sharing. Around 70 per cent of the new jobs which have been created in the UK in the last five years have been neither permanent nor full time. The most common ways of working are now short-term contracts, part-time jobs and self-employment.

The current changes in employment are not going to be reversed. More and more companies now openly admit that they cannot offer jobs for life and we will never return to the days when employment was known as forty-forty – forty hours of paid work per week for forty years with one employer. You have to accept that, unlike your grandparents, whatever your qualifications, it's highly unlikely that you'll remain in the same job all your working life. You will have to regularly re-train and rethink how you work in order to keep up with the new technology and the changing face of employment.

You will have to take more responsibility for how you work, the work that you do, how you find it and when and where you do it. Often change can make us feel apprehensive, but rather than be anxious and worried about the changes in employment, it is more positive to see them as an exciting challenge. They open up new opportunities, making you exploit your skills and talents in a totally new way, often liberating you from a way of work that you disliked and a career path that was going nowhere.

If you are just starting out in the world of work it can seem like a minefield that school, college or university never truly prepared you for. If you are already out there in the workforce then you are wrestling daily with changes which can often feel overwhelming if you aren't in step with them. If you are carrying the scars of recession, knowing that the skills you have are now either performed by robots or not at all, then you need to put your energies into reinventing yourself and what you do. If you are middle aged you may suddenly feel that everyone that you work with is so much younger, that technology is so foreign and that the working knowledge that you have accumulated is now being discarded. You need to find a way of putting your energies into a new career or even redefining what you mean by work. Experience is still valued, but not out-of-date experience. The purpose of this book is to guide you through the changes and equip you for employment in the next century.

AIMS AND OBJECTIVES OF THIS BOOK

The aim of this book is to help you survive in the brave new world of future employment. It will give you a broad world view of work trends, with up-to-the-minute research on jobs, facts and statistics, expert advice and guidance, personal case studies, practical tips and a crisis action plan. The fear is taken out of the future by giving you information on:

- Which jobs are in and which are out so that you know where to focus your training and ensure that you choose an area of employment that's going to grow in the future, not disappear.

- Women and their employment needs, with advice on how to combine work and family.

- Help for unemployed men who have changed roles and recognise the importance of being the main family carer, and how to use this opportunity to re-train.

- The various ways of working, from going part time to taking a sabbatical.

- How to do your own skills audit which will unlock your potential and help you to find which new area of employment you would be successful in.

- Understanding and overcoming techno fear and job stress.

This book will open your eyes to the new employment possibilities and challenges ahead, and arm you with the necessary knowledge to face them successfully.

Because this subject is so large and varied, and the book covers psychological and technical, as well as futuristic aspects of work, it has been divided into four parts for easy reading. Within each part there are a number of chapters. This means that you can either read from beginning to end, discovering and learning as you go, or you can dip into sections and sub-sections that you feel are relevant to your present employment needs.

Part 1: The World of Work

The first section looks at the dramatic changes in employment, because I believe that once you understand the changes, they aren't so frightening. Knowledge gives you back a feeling of control. This in turn gives you optimism and inner strength and provides you with the ability to move forward. Once the changes are understood then you can alter your skills to fit the work requirements. Knowing what these new requirements are means becoming aware of which jobs are in and which jobs are out. There isn't any point in studying for a career which won't exist in the future. There is every advantage to adapting your skills to the employment opportunities which are going to be future front runners.

I cover ageism because it affects both the young and the older worker – older now being defined in some instances as anyone over thirty-five. There are suggestions on how to combat it with a positive approach, which shows in what you say and the way that you say it. I also look at updating your skills, retraining and more flexible ways of working.

Women appear to be well-equipped for the new ways of work, but some men are finding it a hard nut to crack, especially when the job they used to do no longer exists. Understanding your role in the modern working world and how to fit into it is vital for your feeling of self-worth.

Part 2: New Work

This covers a pot pourri of subjects ranging from the new work space and how it affects what you do and where you do it, to the many alternative ways of working, such as flexi-time, self-employment, sabbaticals and downshifting. They all have their dos and their don'ts, their positive and negative aspects, and knowing what these are will help you to make a more educated and correct choice to suit your employment and family needs.

Part 3: Survival Skills

Check your survival rating by answering the quick-fix feedback questionnaire which will give you an opportunity to change your employment perspective. By the time you've finished reading this part you should be able to do a self-selling skills audit. You will discover many talents that you have never recognised before. There is advice on writing your CV, handling job interviews, tips for successful networking and how to prepare for change. It highlights how to identify the causes of stress and how to deal with crisis, giving you a more positive outlook on your work and employment opportunities.

Part 4: Useful Information

This explores the golden nuggets of career changing, job finding and multi-skilling. It contains an appendix of new work jargon so never again will you look confused and fail to understand the new terminology. Plus you will find a list of various useful organisations which will be able to give you more information about specific areas of employment.

MY STORY

I have worked in the media all through my career. What is interesting, and now highly relevant, is that the way people in the media are employed, and the ways in which I have been employed are now becoming universal.

I started out working in the theatre, where I worked my way up to assistant stage manager, then decided to move into advertising as a copywriter. After a few months searching I got an interview and was offered a job with a large, well-known ad agency. I was given a desk, a typewriter and a list of clients and their products, all this when I wasn't even sure how to work the tea machine, let alone type. I quickly learnt the creative rules, wrote the ads and the commercials and, like most people in the industry at that time, moved to another agency every few years, because I wanted a higher salary and greater challenges.

After some time, I felt I wasn't going anywhere. I didn't want to be a creative group head, neither did I want to be an old copywriter. So, I began to talk and, more importantly, to listen to people writing for newspapers and magazines – the area of employment that I wanted to move into. I studied the styles of various writers, read what they wrote and tried to spot gaps in the market and what I could offer to fill them. I decided that working freelance was my only way in. It was also the way an employer would get to know me and my work, and hopefully ask me to do more. I stayed in my job and sent off lots of letters to features editors of magazines and newspapers. I was right to keep my job, as I certainly couldn't have survived financially on the few short stories and articles that I sold.

Eventually, one of these editors suggested I should get myself a literary agent. Using contact addresses and names from the *Writers' & Artists' Yearbook*, I sent off samples of my writing and my CV to various literary agents. I quickly found an agent and it was her job, for a commission, to find me work. She sent me to see the editor of a new magazine who commissioned me to write a piece and then another and finally offered me a contract for a regularly weekly column. At last I felt I could risk giving up my job as a copywriter.

My portfolio career really began in earnest. Through my column I began to get work from newspapers. I started to network and I became known in the industry. One of the national newspapers I was freelancing for suddenly offered me a job as a feature writer. I joined the union and gave up the column. After a few years, impending changes in the world of newspapers made me decide it was time to move on.

My background in journalism indicated that I could make my next career move into television. I knew very little about it apart from how to use the on-off button on my set at home, so I watched a lot of television to see where I could fit into the market. I came up with an idea and instead of writing it up, I tried to sell it to television, together with my transferable skills from journalism such as research, an eye for a story and interviewing techniques.

The first programme editor I discussed my idea with couldn't take it on but advised me to contact someone else and through him I found an editor who gave me a short-term contract – after two programmes the series finished. I decided to go back to the first programme editor that I had spoken to and tell him that I had taken his advice, to show him I hadn't been wasting his time. I would then ask for his advice again. He was very surprised I had actually acted on his suggestion, in his experience, people usually didn't, and he said he could now offer me a job on his programme. When he moved to become one of the heads of commercial television he invited me to go with him, and I worked for many programmes within that company for many years, occasionally still writing freelance articles for newspapers and magazines. It was through one of those freelance articles on sexual harassment at work that a publisher commissioned me to write my first book on the same subject.

Because of changes in the law television programmes began to be made in a totally different way, so I decided to go completely freelance. This is the way that I have been making television programmes and writing books for the last twelve years. I have often worked for more than one employer at the same time in order to survive financially.

I have worked on short-term contracts lasting from six months to a day. I have worked as a full-time employee, I have been self-employed, worked part time on a three-day-a-week basis, been freelance and been an employer. I have worked from home and in office blocks for large organisations. I've done my own tax and invoicing and built relationships with my bank managers. I've learnt the benefits of building a network and negotiating. I have transferred my skills and made sure that in the fast-changing world of technology the skills I need are up to date. I have worked in a team and alone. I have learnt to handle stress through alternative ways of working. I have become assertive in order to be heard and to survive and perhaps, just as importantly, I have made a policy not to forget to laugh at it all.

FACING UP TO NEW TECHNOLOGY

If you are out looking for a job, whether it's your first job or a career change, don't feel daunted by the requirements that the new technology demands. Remember that economic historians point out that new technology has always created more jobs than it has destroyed and there is no collective reason why this shouldn't happen again. History shows that we adapt very quickly to new technology, until most of us can hardly remember the 'old' ways of doing things, while the new generation are only too eager to push back the boundaries.

The events of the 1980s, when a million manufacturing jobs were lost in the UK, provide a perfect example. In stepped technology and just one of the many new computer companies that didn't exist fifteen years ago now directly employs 300,000 people in designing and selling software. Many times that number of people are employed by retailers, specialist magazines, repair and maintenance services, and in user support roles, to enable the product to get to the consumer. Whatever the current economic difficulties of countries where microchips are produced, microchips are here to stay and not only as a vital part of our working lives, but also of our everyday lives, since the cheaper they get the more uses they will have.

IT (information technology) software and information service industries are one of the fastest changing and dynamic sectors of employment, creating many new jobs. Worldwide there are over ten million people working in software industries. IT has proved that it has the potential to have a major impact on the investment and the organisation of work across the global economy. A recent American study showed that increased competition in telecommunications could create over 3 million extra jobs in America over a period of only ten years.

You need to be aware of the way the world of work is moving if you are to thrive in it. All areas of employment are likely to be affected by computers and new technology; if not the machinery, then simply running the business on a daily basis. So catering, construction, engineering, agriculture, retail and leisure industries are all being dragged into the technological age. Have you noticed that even the washing-machine repair man now comes equipped with his own lap-top? The invoice that used to be sent out to you can now be printed out and handed over on the spot.

Even the work itself is on the move. From north to south, east to west, jobs can now be sent down the line, and performed on the other side of the world. You don't even need an office any longer, that inner sanctum full of all those status symbols – who needs it when you can work from an aeroplane seat or your car?

Trying to hold on to the past and doing things the 'old way' will only increase your stress and your personal stagnation. As Valerie Bayliss, Project Director of Redefining Work, at the Royal Society for the Encouragement of Arts, Manufacturers and Commerce recently said, 'The true optimism for the future lies in the fact that this tougher, more competitive world will offer more opportunities. There is footloose investment in the world and it concentrates mainly on the countries with the best-educated, flexible, skilled workforce. There is no reason why you shouldn't be part of that.'

THE ROAD TO EMPLOYMENT

I am convinced that the employment journey isn't such a bumpy ride if you're armed with the necessary information. It is important to realise that you're not alone and that there are lessons to be learnt from the experiences of others. Colleagues and friends have gone through the same employment upheavals and taken up the same challenges. Some of them are in this book, turning their working lives around:

- A teacher who took his redundancy and bought a milk round; another who has opened a sandwich bar; and a science teacher who now has a number of freelance jobs ranging from courier, freelance sourcer using the Internet, plus private tutoring and researcher.

- A television PA who was exhausted from trying to fit the demands of her job, which often meant travelling and working long hours, with the demands of her children. Her love of flowers inspired her to start a business designing floral arrangements for weddings and parties. It is now a highly successful venture and she sees far more of her family than before.

- A nurse who became a social worker and now, after years of training, is a therapist. When she was doing her therapy training she relied on part-time social work to supplement her income. She is now a fully trained therapist with a full patient list and finds her work is both rewarding and also fits in with her family needs.

- A solicitor whose main source of income was from house conveyancing who battled through the recession when house sales slumped. He then sold his business, and took courses in catering and hotel management, and has just opened a small seaside hotel. He says he's never looked back, and describes the change as the biggest and best challenge of his life.

You, too, have probably felt the effects of huge changes in employment across the board in a short space of time, with a recession thrown in just to shake it all about. Like millions of others, you've survived and you've probably found that the learning opportunities have been fantastic. You may have realised that there are certain areas in your field of employment where your skills are no longer in demand because the market has changed and so have you. Of course, if you really wanted to go into that area of employment there is no reason why you shouldn't successfully re-train.

I have experienced a variety of different aspects of work and employment. The flexible ways in which I have worked are today becoming applicable to all areas of employment. Because of this experience I feel that I am now in a suitable position to offer employment advice to others.

CONCLUSION

The key questions you will have to answer in this employment revolution are how to define work, how do you educate yourself in order to be able to work and how will you get that work?

Not all the old methods of surviving and getting a job are being thrown out; they just need updating and reappraising. Your future employment is likely to be much more diverse, so it's important for you to develop a portfolio career; a variety of different skills to enable you to compete in the modern work-place. Like chameleons, we have to be prepared to change and be aware of change. For some that will be easy, for others it will be more uncomfortable. For all of us it will be positive.

Looking for employment is rather like going on a treasure hunt, but you are the main part of the treasure because you have the skills and the talent and the ability to adapt and relearn and re-train. In some instances you may not even yet know that you have such talents and can go for such job opportunities. This is a journey of discovery, so look upon this book as your map.

PART 1

The World of Work

CHAPTER 1

Work Out — Work In

There is a revolution going on in the world of work that many of you will have already experienced first hand, in the form of job losses, re-training and career confusion. Certain types of jobs including many in the service industries, are coming to an end and many others are becoming unrecognisable in the way they function and the products they produce. In order to survive you have to be aware of the changes and change with them.

HISTORY AND CHANGE

The way that we work and the work that we do has changed considerably. What is happening in employment isn't as bad as it may first appear. After all there isn't anything new about changes in the way we work; it's just that in the past changes were local and took time to spread. Now not only are there changes which affect the ways in which we market and merchandise our products, and how we produce and finance them, but also all of this can be communicated and take effect around the world in a very short space of time. If we look back at the history of employment, and it has changed hugely in the last century, we have always embraced change and adapted not only to the way it affected our lives, often for the better, but also the way in which we worked.

Throughout history people have had to re-train and relearn in order to keep pace with change. They have had to adapt to their own new technology; a moving force that invention and progress have never allowed to stand still. For example the invention of the power loom, and the transformation that this brought to steam-driven machines which were able to mass-produce cloth, made huge changes to the efficiency of manufacturing. The result was that production increased, prices fell and new markets opened up around the world. The invention of the internal combustion engine meant that employment among carriage makers fell dramatically, while employment in the car manufacturing industries soared and did so for many years. My father used a typewriter, and I use a computer keyboard, but very soon that too will be extinct because I'll be able to dictate directly to my computer and my words will appear immediately on my computer screen.

THE SPEED OF CHANGE

Because things are moving so fast it isn't possible to accurately predict the speed at which these changes will affect business and industry and your job. In other words, which industries will survive and which will go to the wall. But new technology in the form of the microchip, globalisation and the changing age of the population all offer guidelines as to which areas of employment and business will lead us into the first few years of the millennium and what knock-on effects this will have.

A recent RSA (Royal Society for the encouragement of Arts, Manufacturers and Commerce) report on Redefining of Work suggests that there isn't any point in preparing people for a world that no longer exists. The demands of the 'knowledge society' will be very different from those of the past and it will be people with a good standard of education who will be able to thrive in it. You should concentrate on the new skills – you need to:

• acquire IT capabilities to a high standard

• have an ability to learn new skills and knowledge

- know how to take charge of your own learning

- be able to communicate effectively with others

- be able to work in a team

- know how to manage risk and uncertainty

- know how to manage your own time and get results

- know how to manage your financial affairs

- know how to make the best of your creative talents

- know how to market yourself

- understand self-employment

- become multi-skilled

- find flexible ways of working

- take the opportunities to re-train

- become more assertive and self-confident

- deal with stress and guilt

- understand the death of distance and globalisation and the employment advantages and disadvantages that it brings

- be prepared to change main earner roles with your partner.

The new competencies will be about handling life, as well as employment because the two will merge as more of us work from home, telecommute, work part time and become self-employed. The world of work is uncertain and for many of us an uncomfortable. But change can be exciting and exhilarating, making us see ourselves in a different way, changing our set working patterns, investigating our other talents and taking on board new skills.

I'm convinced that we're all multi-faceted in our employment capabilities, it's just that traditionally employers have only wanted a few of our skills to fit into one job. Now you can di-versify in as many different directions as you want. I think you'll be surprised when you do your skills audit (Chapter 8), and see just how talented you are and just how many transferable skills you have available at your fingertips.

Technology

New technology lies at the root of many of the rapid changes in employment. Many people have seen their jobs taken over by robots and computers and you may be worried that your job is going to go the same way. Microchips are becoming so cheap and readily available they can now be found in something as everyday as birthday cards. There is now far more processing power in a cell phone than there was in the moon landing rockets in the 1960s. In the next decade computers will be a thousand times more powerful and will therefore be capable of doing more than just the mundane tasks that they do today. If the mundane jobs are being done by a machine, then we have to become even more highly skilled because it will only be the highly skilled jobs that will be left for us to do. We also have to be able to use this sophisticated powerful machinery to our advantage.

Microchips produced in countries where labour is cheap have meant that a huge number of labour-intensive jobs and rafts of middle managers in the West have been replaced by inexpensive machines and devices. This trend will continue simply because it's cheaper to employ a machine than it is a person, especially for a job that does not require human skills, and can often be done more efficiently by a machine. Computer chips will soon be in use in almost every aspect of our daily lives, from medical diagnosis to building and maintaining our houses, and from running our companies to designing our products. If it takes one person to work a machine that is doing the job of four people, then the organisation needs fewer employees. The middle managers who were the go-betweens are also not needed, and the company hierarchy structure is automatically broken down. Managers have already felt huge changes in the way that they work, taking on more immediate responsibility without support staff which results in them having to deal with their own correspondence by using a PC.

Globalisation

This knock-on effect is very important and although you may not think, for example, that low earth orbit world-wide satellites, which are now in operation, are relevant to you and your work, they are. Once they are in position it means that you will be able to use a satellite phone anywhere in the world, however remote – even from Mount Everest. Plus, you will have high speed access via satellite to be able to use your phone and lap top in places such as India and Africa which at the moment are too expensive to cable up. When we open up the Third World to global communications this changes the way we do business. For example, postal communications will decrease and this will affect airline business, not to mention the trade and the outsourcing (see Chapter 2) which we'll be able to do with these countries.

IT'S VIRTUALLY HERE

One of the biggest buzz phrases of the 1990s is the 'virtual organisation'. We already have the virtual office (see Chapter 5), and people are already able to hold virtual meetings. The new technology allows people to meet, not face to face in one place, but using the Internet, sometimes communicating with people in other countries via a satellite link. There are many successful organisations, such as airline booking facilities and insurance companies, which are now employing only a handful of people and using new technology to service customers all over the world.

What the virtual organisation already means is that you will no longer have to move people around for them to be able to come together and work as a team. This is especially relevant in organisations where team work is spasmodic. For example, where freelance people are brought in for a specific project such as the launch of a new product, and advertising, packaging, marketing and consumer research people need to be brought together for brainstorming or sharing of information. Already distances are being reduced and, with a PC or a network computer and a variety of linkage options, people can work with each other anywhere. If you have specialist skills and work for a number of different clients and cannot afford to spend time travelling between them, then this type of communication is ideal. Equally, if you work for an organisation where there have been staff cuts and you now have a larger work load, not having to leave your desk to travel to a meeting can be very beneficial. For home workers this type of meeting and communication is a huge boon in time saving.

Is it really science fiction to imagine that in the near future there won't be any humans in the company boardroom, only computers? Organisations will require fewer managers and those that remain will be more hands-on. Decisions made by machines will be based on facts and research, not on emotions or tradition. If the machine decides that it should close one of its branches, then it will close it. If you are heading for a career in management then you must be sure that you are capable of working hands-on and performing more than just hierarchy management tasks. You must also be capable of making decisions based on factual information, working with the new technology, not against it.

WORK OUT – WORK IN

If you are looking for employment or changing your career, winding down your level of employment or winding up at the start of your working life, it's important to have some idea of which areas of work are changing and which are expected to flourish and grow.

US employment projections until 2006 expect employment to continue to rise, but that rise will not be spread evenly across all types of work or across all areas of the world. Full-time employment is unlikely to increase, while part-time work is already becoming the employment of the future. Currently, one in ten of Britain's 27 million workers are losing their jobs and it is predicted that this situation will continue over the next three years.

Forecasting organisations are not only able to predict which areas of employment will change in the future, but they also offer facts and figures, so that we are able to see at a glance the statistical changes that have already taken place and how it is predicted these changes will continue. This can help you to make decisions about your career in terms of training and job changing. Armed with such information decisions become easier to make and more reliable.

Work Out

We have seen that many factors are changing the face of employment, causing some jobs to diminish and others to thrive and grow. If you are considering training for a job, are already working in a declining industry or want to know how you can use your existing skills to move to a new career, then the lists below show you which direction to take and where to look for employment. Here are just some of the areas of employment that have been affected by change and that employment specialists forecast to be on the decline.

Manufacturing

In 1981 there were nearly 6 million people in the UK employed in manufacturing; in 1998 the figure stands at a little over 4 million (Business Strategies Economic forecasting group). The decline in manufacturing has partly been affected by outsourcing, where the same job can be done more cheaply in an area or even a country where jobs are scarce and overheads cost less. It's thought that the manufacturing industry could fall from 16 per cent of the employment market in 1996 to 14 per cent by 2006. The Fortune 500 industrial companies in the US employed 3.7 million fewer workers in 1991 than in 1981, a loss of about one job in four. This trend is expected to get worse in the next century taking into account outsourcing, new technological forms of communication and flatter management structures.

Basic Clerical and Secretarial

Between 1996 and 2006 basic clerical and secretarial posts are expected to decline by 25,000 jobs, according to the US Bureau of Labor Statistics. This is because new technology and forms of communication have already taken over many of these jobs, together with outsourcing. The new technology also means that many managers now do their own secretarial work.

Middle Managers and business administrators
These jobs have already been hit badly because the traditional job of middle managers in large organisations was to pass information up and down the employment hierarchy. Now, organisations have computer networks and more open, flatter structures. These provide people with information and an ability to organise their own work structure without the use of a middle manager.

Agricultural, forestry and fishing
It is predicted by the US Bureau of Labor Statistics that these occupations will halt in their decline in employment from the previous fifteen-year period (1975 to 1990), but will only increase by 5 per cent from 1990 to 2005.

Prototype workers
Occupations using trained skills and judgement such as tool makers and prototype workers are expected to see relatively large falls of employment of around 120,000 between 1996 and 2006 (US Bureau of Labour Statistics). This is because computer-controlled tools can achieve the same degree of skill.

Manual jobs
In 1981 manual jobs – both skilled and unskilled – made up almost a third of the total employment in the UK economy, but by 1996 that had fallen to 22.4 per cent (Business Strategies economic forecasting group). By 2006 the proportion will have dropped to 20 per cent. The fall will particularly hit the North of England and Scotland. In Australia between 1994 and 1998 manual jobs only increased by 10 per cent, in the US it is projected that between now and 2006 this type of employment will only increase by 8 per cent.

Other

Construction workers, miners, plant/machine operatives, tool makers, transport workers, travelling sales representatives and those working for the utilities are also seeing the number of jobs decline.

Work In

The good news is that the period between 1996 to 2006 will be a period of steady employment growth. By 2006 it is expected that employment will have risen to nearly 27 million. Because of the new technology, an ageing population and a rising female work-force there will be almost 1.6 million extra jobs in the economy in 2006 compared to 1996.

For social as well as technological reasons, many new areas of employment are blossoming. For example, the ageing popula-tion is producing a ground swell of employment because not only do many of them require different forms of care, but also many older people have considerable spending power. The continuing increase in the numbers of working women is also creating a burgeoning industry in all areas of child care, plus the new technology has created more leisure time. Don't overlook small scale organisations – in the US some 80 per cent of new jobs have been created by small and medium-scale enterprises and this is reflected in many developing countries as well as in Europe (International Labour Organisation). Listed below are just some of the areas of employment that are predicted to rise.

Professional, Managerial and Technical

Recent projections by the US Bureau of Labor Statistics show that the fastest growth rates are expected in these occupations. They are expected to increase on average by 2.4 per cent annu-ally between 1996 and 2001, and to represent almost two in every five jobs by 2006.

The number of jobs in the UK for managers, scientists, doctors, nurses, teachers, computer experts, legal executives and other professionals has risen from 8.7 million in 1991 to 9.2 million last year and is set to rise to 10.5 million by the year 2006

(Business Strategies economic forecasting group). This figure is also reflected in other Western countries and is a result of the increase in the ageing population, the use of IT in work and and leisure, and the increase in the use of the law to settle both personal and employment disputes. Between 1996 and 2006 in the UK, half the increase in employment will be in the area of self-employment and the other half by additional part-time jobs.

Service Sector

Another growth area is service sector employment which is expected to continue to rise, increasing its share of total employment from 46 per cent in 1996 to 49 per cent in 2006. This is because third world countries can manufacture goods cheaper than Western countries, which has turned Western employment (including the UK), from manufacturing to service providing. Most workers in the West now provide a service not a product.

Office Staff

Experienced, multi-skilled PA secretaries at director level come top of the list of staff categories where demand has outstripped supply. In Australia, over the last four years the demand for multi-skilled office staff has increased by 23 per cent (Australian Government Statistics). According to a recent survey by a group of British employment agencies, 19 per cent of employers specifically identified the following skills shortages at this level:

- Fast shorthand speeds are in demand for secretaries.
- There is a shortage of secretaries with foreign language skills.
- IT skills are the main requirement for office workers at all levels.

As in all other areas of employment secretaries have to become more highly skilled in order to survive. They are now expected to have higher qualifications such as faster keyboard speeds, a full knowledge of the new information technology and an ability to speak one or more foreign languages. The basic office skills can now be performed by the new technology, an office junior or even by a management person. If you want to be a secretary you must make sure that you are as highly skilled as possible.

Knowledge Workers

New jobs are likely to be found in skilled, intensive, knowledge based occupations. An increase in higher level of qualifications will be needed to match the changes. The biggest employment growth since 1981 has been in computers and related jobs. The US Bureau of Labor Statistics has projected an increase of 103 per cent in systems analysts by the year 2006.

The south of England will continue to dominate in computer software and support jobs, while other regions will lag behind. There will be an extra 500,000 'knowledge workers' in the south-east of England by 2006, while the whole of the West Midlands will only see another 80,000 jobs created.

According to statistics from the US Bureau of Labor, demand for IT workers will rise by 1.3 million over the next ten years in the US alone. There is already a severe shortage of IT skills worldwide, doing jobs such as:

- data processing equipment repairs
- electronic pagination systems workers
- computer programming
- equipment repairs

Both in the UK and in America the salaries of IT workers have risen rapidly in the last few years. Between 1995 and 1996 they rose by 20 per cent. Research shows that computer network professionals' salaries increased between 1996 and 1997 by an average of 7.4 per cent. The US Government predicts that by 2006 employment for computer specialists will have increased by 118 per cent.

Coming of Age

The population of the world is ageing. There are currently well over three-quarters of a million people over retirement age continuing to work in the UK. This amount is forecast to increase marginally to 839,000 by 2001. Between 1996 and 2001 the number of people of working age over thirty-five will increase by 9 per cent. Between now and 2040 the ageing population – that's those aged sixty-five and upwards – will increase by 53 per cent (statistics from the US Social Security Administration).

In the West we are now living longer and staying healthier, so there are more workers and more consumers in the marketplace. The ageing population of the Western world, many of whom have spending power, will in itself create employment in specific areas such as:

- care of the elderly, in residential homes, warden assisted homes, home care, home help, full nursing care
- leisure, holidays, fitness, golfing, health, beauty, surgery, all specifically aimed at the elderly
- biology and medical care aimed at the elderly
- home health aids, disability aids and security

Working Women

Working women have also been affected by changes in employment, because their working history has taken such huge strides in the twentieth century. Before the First World War women hardly ever worked outside of the home. Middle- and upper-class women were brought up to sew, have children and 'be a wife'. In my mother's passport she wrote that her profession was 'being a wife': this wasn't a matter of pride, it was simply a matter of fact. Today almost half of the workforce in Britain is made up of women, probably more if you took into account the black economy and the caring jobs women do which they aren't paid for. The numbers of women in employment have increased despite the fact that that they are often having to juggle between having a career and being the main family carer, and in many instances the main family earner as well.

The good news for women who want to work is that by 2001 they are expected to make up 45 per cent of the labour force compared to just 39 per cent in 1976. Women are much more prepared to work part time and are attracted by the increasing flexibility of work, because frequently this fits in with their family and care commitments. Out of the total number of new job opportunities that will be created in the coming years, two-thirds of them will be taken up by women.

Although the increase that we are already seeing in the numbers of working women is to be found in flexible areas of employment such as part-time working, the three major fastest growing highly skilled occupational groups for women are:

- executive
- administrative and managerial
- professional specialities, and technicians and related support

These groups require the highest level of education, and also have workers with the highest proportion of degrees and the highest earnings when compared with other major groups (see Chapter 4).

REINVENTING YOURSELF

This is a time of change and challenge where employment is being stood on its head. As long as you are prepared for the change then you can face the challenge, and challenges are frequently exciting and stimulating, giving you the opportunity to learn, explore and use your many skills and talents. Change is part of reinventing yourself and you must be prepared to change your career not just once, but according to the predictions of some UK employment analysts, at least three or four times, or in America eleven times, during your working life. Experts agree that if you are working in areas of high technology, where the very tools of your trade are always changing and moving forward, then you must be prepared to go back to college or in some way learn new skills, at a minimum of every five to ten years. If you are one of those people whose skills are limited within one area of employment, which for whatever reason now no longer exists, you will have to do a skills audit on yourself (see Chapter 8) and explore your other talents in terms of new employment opportunities. A year after losing their jobs 46 per cent of UK coal miners were still unemployed and those who did find work saw their pay drop by an average of 30 per cent. However, secretaries have done well from the employment revolution by reinventing themselves as PAs (personal assistants), researchers, IT specialists and personnel and data managers.

Here are some old areas of employment which are developing into something new:

Old Job	New Job
Bank note printer	*Smart card designer (*someone who designs credit cards or security cards with a microchip in them)
Bank clerk	*Call centre agent* (someone who deals with customers or sales calls over the telephone)
Company worker	*Portfolio worker* (someone who works for more than one employer)
Training manager	*Development consultant* (someone who advises organisations on how to expand)
Steel worker	*Control technician* (someone who monitors production processes)
Draughtsman	*CAD operator* (someone who uses Computer Assisted Design techniques)
Ambulance driver	*Paramedic* (someone who drives an ambulance but is also trained in first aid and resuscitation procedures)

(list from the RSA Redefining Work Project)

CONCLUSION

The message is don't be too narrow with your job search. Widen your net. Look at how your area of employment has changed and spread in all directions; you need to try and be part of that change.

In order to achieve that you must be prepared to:

• re-train

• change your career, not just your job

• discuss your situation with a careers counsellor

• look at the skills you have used and those you may not even be aware that you have

- logically map out how you can utilise your skills towards future employment

- remember that many of your skills will overlap into other employment areas.

You may have to see yourself working in a different area altogether (see Chapter 6), but once you have made the mental jump, the physical leap of re-training and re-evaluating isn't so difficult.

Your employment potential lies in your future. From your employment past you can take your expertise and your experience, and start a whole new career.

CHAPTER 2

The Changing World of Work

If you live in an area where employment opportunities are thin on the ground then the wonders of the shrinking world of work, brought about by the new technology, can alter your job chances. The reason for this is because of fibre optics and sophisticated electronics that make up the telephone lines. So that just as phone calls can be passed around the world, so now can Internet and computer activities, because they both use the same telephone technology. The capacity of the main telephone trunk lines has increased much faster than the growth in voice traffic, which is why the price of making a phone call has fallen. According to the World Bank by the year 2010, the cost of making a transatlantic call will have dropped to under 2 pence an hour. Because of this low cost it is now possible for services that can be carried out down the phone lines to be delivered as easily and cheaply from Calcutta as they can from Catford. The only difference is that the worker in Calcutta is probably paid less. In order to compete with this you have to be more highly skilled and be able to speak more than one language, although of course English speakers are lucky in that English continues to be the universal language of work.

This abolition of distance, which is moving international trade around the world – known as off-shore dumping – is something we've probably all been consumers of, but probably not realised it. When you dial a number on your phone from London you have no idea just where the person at the other end of the line may be talking to you from. So you wouldn't know, for example, that the freephone number shown on various television advertisements has been re-routed out of England to one of the many thousands of operators in Colorado and Utah in America.

Staff in call centres (see Chapter 6) in Newcastle in the UK are also being trained to handle overflow calls from America. In order to be able to handle calls from the Asian community living in America, companies are considering using telecommuting centres in the Far East. There is a lot of cross-fertilisation of jobs in this field, and this is becoming more popular with organisations that straddle time zones, want to cut out high street outlets and reduce their overheads. Owing to the breakdown in different languages and cultures, more of this type of employment is criss-crossing the world, bringing all of us wider job opportunities.

GLOBALISATION

Global Communications

One of the advantages of global communications is that it is now being thought of as a way of keeping highly skilled workers in their own home country, rather than them going abroad for employment and taking their skills elsewhere. For example, film specialists are electronically transferring digital film between companies for viewing and editing by using a direct connection between England and Hollywood. Film rushes can cross the Atlantic with the speed of light – and because London is working while Los Angeles is asleep, producers will be able to see how the film is progressing day by day. It is hoped that this form of working will keep highly skilled people in a wide range of areas – such as animation, graphics, special effects, make-up and film technicians – employed at home.

Shifting Jobs

According to the World Bank the globalisation of employment could mean that within a single generation there will be a highly competitive global tele-economy, with a rat race for competitiveness. This could either be good news for third world countries, or we might see a repeat of the sweatshops of the textile industry. On the other hand the skills learnt by women in the Caribbean, for example, could help them to create a more highly skilled information service in the future, resulting in a highly trained resource base. Certainly it will decentralise a lot of jobs that previously only provided work because of their geographical position. For example, in the not too distant future it will be possible to transmit and switch video signals without overloading networks, then a whole new range of employment opportunities will open up for developing countries. For example, the World Bank has already trialed the idea of security cameras in American shopping malls being monitored by people in Africa.

If you live in an area of high unemployment, shifting jobs could bring work to your doorstep, which was previously performed elsewhere. You should be aware though that this type of employment is not particularly high paid.

Exporting Office Work

Voice telephone work is only a small part of the traffic that rushes around the international telephone network. Much more of it is data, such as documents, graphics, photographs and videos, all of them digitised or translated into the language of computers because digital material can be exported or imported easily.

Exporting office work started twenty-five years ago, when American insurance companies began sending claims forms to the Caribbean to be typed. First the forms went by ship, then by plane, now they are sent down the line. Offshore work can differ between low status relatively mechanical work, like data entry (which is inputting text or data via a keyboard), to high status information processing.

We have to be aware that work isn't any longer something that happens locally, and that what happens in the shrinking world of work often affects us. In this instance if you want to get a job in this area of employment and there is plenty of it around then it is important to realise that repetitive data entry work is often done in countries where the labour costs are extremely low. For example, the Philippines is ranked the leader in remote data entry work. The country's major edge lies in its relatively low manpower cost (data entry clerks in America charge $65 for 10,000 key strokes, while the going rate in the Philippines is between $4 to $6 for the same number of keystrokes).

Workers in other countries – Jamaica, Korea, Malaysia, Mexico, Sri Lanka and Cyprus – are able to do this work cheaply, so you have to make sure that you are more highly skilled than they are and can do high status information processing, which is big business both in the UK, the US and Europe. For example, one leading American insurance company gets about 4,000 medical claims forms processed each day by 120 staff in Loughrea, in the Republic of Ireland.

If this area of employment appeals to you then you must make sure that you have the right communication skills, up-to-date keyboard skills and that you are fully qualified to use all the new types of technology on the market in order to compete. But be aware that this type of work is repetitious and is not career based. The competion for cheap labour in other countries makes this type of work fairly low paid here.

COMPANY RELOCATION

Many companies and organisations are seeing the advantages of relocating. In other words geographically shifting their employment base from metropolitan areas where the rents and leases are expensive, competition is high and it's hard to attract a skilled and motivated workforce, to areas where the competition is less, the rents and leases are low and space is available to have offices built to their special requirements.

But what employment opportunities does this bring to you?

If you live in an area where unemployment is high and job opportunities are few and far between, then a company relocating can bring huge employment opportunities. This work is often in call centres, which isn't usually highly paid, nor does it offer great career opportunities, but the working hours tend to be flexible, commuting is local and many organisations offer job training. Many more organisations are also choosing to relocate, offering work in mail order, spare machinery parts, packaging and clerical work for the banking and finance industry.

Don't forget that when companies relocate they attract other subsidiary employment. For example, sandwich bars, taxi services, garages, pubs and local corner shops all offer support services and bring new employment. This brings all sorts of alternative job opportunities which could fit your existing skills or you could look to re-train. Remember also that company relocation can also bring work opportunities for the self-employed such as a sandwich round, child care and nursery teaching opportunities. In order to remain competitive, brush up on your skills, be adaptable and look for new employment opportunities.

DOWNSIZING

It used to be believed that a job is a birthright, something that we are as entitled to as air to breathe and water to drink. That was until there was downsizing. Now a job for life isn't any longer on offer and downsizing, which has swept through companies from the UK to Japan, has turned employment on its head, throwing out the old rules.

To put downsizing into perspective we need to look at the 1970s when businesses wanted to be corporations and corporations wanted to build empires. The bosses wanted big profits, bonuses and cars, and the icing on the corporate cake was a large workforce. Corporate office buildings were huge. Expense account lunches were long. Someone was employed to do the company photocopying, someone else to simply take phone messages.

Then came downsizing. Companies all over the world began to downsize, rationalise or restructure – whatever you want to call it – when they worked out that if two people could be made to do what it previously took three, the cost savings were obvious.

Downsizing is a management philosophy that says that the best and the quickest way to cut a company's costs and increase its market is to axe staff. Everyone suffered, either directly or indirectly. The trend spread relentlessly – anorexic, slimmer, leaner, fitter – these were no longer ways of describing fashion models but of newly downsized companies.

The paternalistic employer who trained and nurtured his employees, and felt as if he was cutting off a limb when he had to 'let them go' was immediately replaced by macho managers who became known as corporate assassins. Respect for skills, expertise and loyalty went out of the boardroom window.

In so many countries, downsizing started from economic necessity, but then became part of the new corporate culture. When the upturn from the recession came, the jobs carried on being cut. Now, 90 per cent of large companies have reorganised and axed staff. One of the beneficial effects of this phenomenon is that the social stigma that used to go with redundancy has disappeared. It hardly exists, simply because at the height of downsizing so many people from all areas of industry, commerce and management and from all social classes, the shop floorworker to the managing director, were affected. Unemployment swept through companies without discretion. Shop floorworkers realised that their jobs had gone to the new technology, and managing directors realised that their company perks had gone forever.

PETER IS forty and he has worked for the same chemical firm for twenty years. He started as an office junior, writing in ledgers and counting out quantities by hand. In the last ten years new technology and downsizing have started squeezing the workforce. Peter watched while a lot of the production staff – especially the middle managers – were made redundant, and secretarial staff were replaced by PCs.

When Peter joined the company there were 340 workers, now there's 140, and he thinks that number will be reduced by the end of this year. 'In the first big chunk of redundancies in the late 1980s, early 1990s all the salesmen left and were replaced by PCs and a modem, so that orders could be taken and product information given down the line. Then the area offices were closed. The next set of purges were four or five years ago.' The company was downsizing in order to save costs, letting new technology replace the workforce.

Peter survived downsizing, although he had to learn to handle the guilt of survivors' syndrome (Chapter 10) and now finds he is working for a much smaller organisation with far more responsibility. In terms of his CV his additional work experience and responsibility can only be a future employment plus. He has gone on all the training and IT courses that the company have offered him and when he feels confident to change jobs, these skills will be transferable to future employment.

We have all had to adjust in one way or another. For some it has been a struggle to come to terms with the employment changes, as families split and whole areas became economically destitute, especially when factories, workshops and white collar companies employing the middle classes, who had survived previous recessions, also closed.

The positive news is that downsizing often liberates people from a job they dislike, allowing them to look at new employment opportunities and to make career changes. It gives you the opportunity to sharpen your skills, be more inventive with your employment possibilities, review your talents and broaden your job search. It has made finding employment more challenging and you now know that having a job is more than just a social right. You have to be more competitive and be prepared to train in areas that previously you might not have even considered you were capable of working in, and finding new approaches to seeking and staying in employment.

DEALING WITH REDUNDANCY

The stark reality is that in this changing climate most of you can expect to be made redundant at least once during your working life. Therefore it's important to be aware of how to survive. Here are some basic golden rules to remember in order to survive redundancy. Some of them aren't easy; you're going to have to work on yourself and be positive.

1. Don't take it personally   Don't ever say 'It's all my fault.' The truth is that you were just another figure on the company balance sheet. Letting you go wasn't ever a comment on your expertise, skills, team work, abilities, working practice or personality; it was a comment on your employer's workplace philosophy, the state of the markets, and the profit and loss sheet.

2. Don't be ashamed, you are not alone   Redundancy no longer has any social stigma attached to it, it's happened to too many people like you, with talent, energy and skills.

3. Don't lie about being made redundant   Be honest on your CV, or when you go for an interview. The person interviewing you may well have been made redundant too, will have interviewed a lot of other people who have been made redundant or may have been in the position of having to make workers redundant. Whatever the scenario, they are very likely to understand your circumstances. Redundancy flooded a lot of highly skilled, experienced workers out on to the job market. If you don't come clean, then you could tie yourself up in knots if you have to tell lies.

4. Value yourself   If you believe that you are what you do, then when you are unemployed and not doing anything workwise, you will start to believe that you are nothing. This feeling of nothingness and low self-worth can easily lead to depression. You have to believe that you are a person in your own right and that your friends and your family care about you for who you are, not what you do. You have many other talents apart from those linked to your employment, talents you may not yet have used or even been aware of.

5. Do your own DIY skills audit   This will help you find out what career changes you can make and what talents you have yet to explore in yourself. You'll find that you have a number of skills that you use every day that you haven't even considered could be transferred to a new type of employment. Don't just look at what you think you are good at, look at what others think you're are good at too. Ask them, they'll be only too happy to tell you. Friends, family and work colleagues can be helpful, but make sure any suggestions about your skills and talents are unbiased (see Chapter 8).

6. See yourself as being multi-skilled   Start to think about having a number of roles, rather than one job. Realise that you can earn from more than one source. You can be employed by more than one person. Part-time, freelance and self-employment make this possible. The more small jobs you have, each one earning you an amount of money, the income will all add up.

7. Explore your options, explore yourself   Take this as an opportunity to re-train, to update your skills and build new networks. Try to expand your skills and become more highly skilled. Highly skilled workers are much in demand and are highly paid. Learning one skill can lead you to another.

8. Consider the alternatives   Perhaps it's time to relocate or trade down for a slower, gentler lifestyle. After all you do have a job of work, and that's finding work.

9. Look at your employment past   Decide if you are working in an area that is a 'sunset industry' or if you are an 'endangered species' (see Chapter 1). In other words, check if the work that you do no longer exists, has been given over to technology or is very rare. If this applies to you then widen your employment search. Whatever you do, from making ice-cream to painting tiles, remember you are a service provider.

10. Be flexible   Be prepared to make a career change, even if that means moving to a totally new area of employment or geographically relocating. Always include your partner and family in these decisions, as it will affect them all. Their needs are as great as yours, and you are part of a team. Your family are sure to be understanding of your emotional as well as your practical needs. Be more flexible in the way that you work, where you can work, the work that you can do and with the skills that you have.

11. Be responsible for your own employment potential   You have the skills, now find the opportunities to use them. You have the ability to change direction, for even if it feels as though you are taking a step backwards, you'll soon be moving forwards again. Don't rely on someone else to find you a job. Look sideways as well as just in front. Don't look behind to regret, only for positive feedback.

12. New technology   Make sure you are up to date with the new technology for either your present career or any areas of employment you are considering moving into. Technology is moving fast, so this isn't easy, but read your trade journals, talk to colleagues in the industry and try to find out what's coming next, so that in an interview situation you understand what they're talking about and are able to answer any questions. It's the one time when you can be a real 'clever clogs'.

13. Re-train   Be prepared to fund your own re-training or updating of skills. Always take any training that is offered to you by your present or future employer, even if it seems a waste of time, or irrelevant, as you'll be surprised how many skills are transferable. The added advantage is that the employer will pay for the course and pay you while you learn.

14. See a careers analyst   They can be positively helpful, especially if you are feeling confused and entrenched.

15. Seek advice from head hunters   Depending on your business head hunters are worth a visit, as they know what's moving in your particular area and who is looking for what.

LIFE AFTER DOWNSIZING

There are many employment opportunities out there; the skill is how to go about finding them (see Chapter 1). Try and identify growth industries by networking (see Chapter 9) and reading trade journals aimed at employment areas you are interested in. Business articles in both local as well as national newspapers, will give you information about what is going on in your own area and the movement within companies and corporations. Look for companies that are keeping pace with change – those within existing industries that best adapt to the new information technologies. Join appropriate trade organisations.

Be aware of what is in and what is out, which businesses are coming and which are going. Know what the competition is doing. Look at job advertisements in newspapers, job centres and journals, see what skills they want and what salaries they are offering. Check what qualifications they require, what age limits they are setting, see whether it's worth you moving to a different area.

It would certainly seem to be the case that even after downsizing has been carried to its logical – or illogical – extreme, and the layoffs and early retirements have stopped, the corporate giants are not going to go back to hiring large numbers of long-term employees. Company bosses have discovered that it is more efficient and profitable to operate as contracting centres, in other words buying in goods and services from smaller companies, rather than having them produced by their own employees, a process known as 'outsourcing'. However, even though many companies now outsource they still have to retain a core of employees and in the future these people will have to:

• be prepared to be employed on short-term contracts

• be hired on a temporary, part-time basis

• work for fees rather than salaries.

The good news, if you are working on this basis, is that if an employer is satisfied with you, you will be rehired, and you will find that one short-term contract can overlap another as you build up a pool of employers seeking your services. You may even find yourself busier than ever before!

If you are asked to work for a fee rather than a salary ask an accountant, relevant trade union or trade journal what the set rates of pay are, or phone up the competition. Contact several companies in the same business and behave as if you are a customer (see Chapter 9). Ask what their charges are and what they expect for that. In this way you'll get some idea of the average market rates. Be bold.

CHAPTER 3

Lifting the Age Barrier

My father retired from full-time employment when he was sixty-five and for a further ten years the firm kept him on in a part-time capacity. Eventually he was only working for two days a week. He enjoyed it; it made him feel that he was still part of the workday routine, travelling to and from the office, being part of the audience for the working day gossip, if not a prime player. He was also still able to do the work as the new technology didn't directly affect his area of employment. Unbelievable as it may seem, this was only ten years ago. Today, none of us can expect to be working into our retirement, let alone into our seventies, in fact there are organisations who consider anyone over forty as being 'too old'.

During the recession and downsizing of the 1980s older workers tended to be the group most affected, because it was thought that offering them early retirement or early redundancy was seen to be more acceptable to everyone. I'm sure it was, because many people over fifty had seen their jobs change beyond recognition and were only too pleased to accept early retirement.

Over the last ten years older workers in countries such as France, Germany, the US and Sweden have all found it difficult to find employment. We should all be aware that the so-called 'grey ceiling' that didn't exist twenty years ago when it was common for people aged between fifty and sixty to be part of the workforce, is with us today. As the post-war 'baby boomer' generation pass fifty there will be more older people than ever before – the number aged between fifty-five and sixty-four is projected to increase in 2006 by over three quarters of a million from their 1996 level (Labour Force Survey). People will not only be living longer but will be more active, in fact, it's predicted that by 2050 the average life expectancy in western Europe could rise to eighty-seven years for women and eighty-three years for men. The simple fact that there will be a greater number of older workers and fewer younger ones coming on to the employment market, because people are having fewer children, will mean that older workers will have to rejoin the workforce.

AGE DISCRIMINATION

A Gallup survey for Age Concern in the UK shows that a quarter of workers have encountered age discrimination at work. Surprisingly half said it was because they were considered to be too young and not ready to settle in a job, the risk being that they would take the training offered and leave to work elsewhere, and that they were also unable to take on job responsibility. And employees in their mid-thirties and forties who say that they have been passed over for training or promotion are convinced it's because of their age. The most common age range for employers to offer training seems to be to those aged between twenty and thirty, but for those aged thirty or over, the likelihood of being re-trained diminishes yearly. In some areas of employment, being over thirty-five, which is only a third of the way into your working life, is considered to be too 'old'. There are areas of employment such as financial trading where the pressure is high and the going is tough, and those in their mid twenties have a high burn-out rate due to stress (see Chapter 10).

The organisation Age Concern found that 18 million British adults have experienced age discrimination in employment, health or welfare, and 79 per cent of workers aged over fifty believed they had been turned down for a job on the grounds of their age, even though they had the right skills and qualifications.

THIS WAS the experience of Judith, a fifty-year-old marketing executive who recently went for an interview with a multinational corporation. 'I had all the right experience and qualifications for the job,' she says, 'The interview went well, they didn't ask me my age.' It went so well that Judith was offered the job on the spot and asked when she could begin. 'We discussed a start date and negotiated a salary.' Judith was told that the contracts department would call her the following day to finalise everything, 'Walking back to the lift I was casually asked if I had young children to look after, as the working hours would be long. I said that my eldest son was in his early thirties, so this wouldn't be a problem. As I said this I noticed their expressions changed and suddenly they became very unfriendly, glanced anxiously at one another and hardly said goodbye.' Judith never heard anything from the company again. 'I'm sure that when they worked out my age from the age of my son, they decided I was too old. There was no other reason why I shouldn't have heard from them. I lost the job.'

Judith should not have mentioned her family situation until she knew the job was signed and sealed, and that she was fully employed. She should also have consulted her nearest Citizens' Advice Bureau or her relevant trade union or trade association for advice on what to do and and to see if she had a legal case for discrimination.

Judith's experience is not unusual, and there have been many reports in the last ten years showing that age discrimination leads to skills shortages and that millions of older workers have justifiable grievances. Even personnel managers, who are generally aware of the dangers of discrimination, have their prejudices. In an IPD survey they said that they believed older workers are generally more effective but less adaptable than younger ones. Moreover, the younger personnel managers viewed older staff less favourably in both productiveness and compatibility. And age discrimination is easily disguised. For example, discounting a job applicant who is a graduate because they are 'over qualified' for the job, and older employees as having 'more qualifications than the job demands', are ways of hiding age discrimination.

There have been calls for legislation to ban age discrimination in the UK, following the lead of other countries. In the US employers cannot discriminate against workers aged between forty and seventy in hiring, discharging, levels of pay, promotion and training opportunities and fringe benefits. French law forbids age limits in job advertisements or making employees redundant because of their age. The government in the UK has said it prefers a voluntary code of practice to deal with ageism in employment, but it seems that attitudes may well prove hard to change.

GETTING BACK TO WORK

Many governments, employers and trade unions are finding that early retirement is not cost effective, and it also tends to un-balance and de-skill the workforce. This is why many employers are now trying to find ways of reversing this trend, offering an assortment of schemes.

Around the world different countries are taking different approaches to older workers. In France, for example, they are experimenting with part-time job sharing, to encourage people who are fifty-five and over to take partial retirement while still receiving 90 per cent of their full-time salary. In Sweden, where the retirement age is relatively late at sixty-five, they have brought in gradual retirement. In Japan many people continue working after the pension age of sixty or sixty-five and some-times older, usually working part time or in a subsidiary firm of their previous employer. They don't earn as much as they would have done before, but what they do earn is on top of their pension. Strong state incentives encourage enterprises to extend working lives in Japan, where good health and levels of life expectancy are among the best in the world.

It seems that slowly employment for older workers is becoming easier. For example, one multinational insurance company has recognised that letting go of too many of their older employees has left a gaping hole in their workforce. They have just interviewed over 1,000 of the workers that they had recently made redundant, to ask them if they wanted to rejoin the company. Most of these people were pleasantly surprised to be contacted by their former employer and offered a job. The end result was that a core of potential re-recruits with basic skills and motivation were re-hired.

There are signs that employers are interested in hiring people who have done a similar job in the same industry and that experience is beginning to matter more than qualifications. The positive message is not to underestimate your experience. This includes not only your years of paid work but also any unpaid work you may do such as running a home, working for a voluntary organisation, spare-time activities or hobbies. Many of the skills that you have developed over the years in all sorts of areas – people skills, people management, driving, organising – things that you probably just take for granted are often exactly what employers are looking for. Skills are transferable and you will be surprised how you can use and adapt them to a completely new work context.

If you are an older worker, remember:

- you may not necessarily find employment in the same area that you have worked in before, so spread your net wide

- there are many options now available in the way that you can work such as part time, job sharing and self-employment

- pick organisations that are openly encouraging the employment of 'older' workers, including many supermarkets, DIY specialists, garden centres and charity outlets.

AGE AND THE INTERVIEW

When you go for a job interview, remember that age shows, and not just in the way that you dress, although it's advisable not to wear clothes that are fifteen years too young for you or fifteen years too old; it sounds obvious but be smart and modern. But it isn't just what you wear that comes across as ageing, far more important is your attitude and what you say and the way that you say it. Older people can sometimes have a ponderous walk and fixed views that are backward looking, which means they can come across to others as being inflexible with little enthusiasm for new things.

Youth presents a lively mind, and is enthusiastic, positive and easily adaptable. You need to sparkle with energy, have a fresh attitude and a smile, a smile takes years off us all.

The chart below shows you a few key phrases that you should use at an interview and those that you should avoid:

Do say phrases like	Don't say phrases like
I am experienced in this type of work, and there is no reason why I can't learn to do it the new way	I am too old to learn anything new
I wasn't trained to do this kind of work, but I am very open minded to new ideas	This is what I was trained to do and I don't know anything else
I'm happy to organise and, if necessary, subsidise my own re-training	My CV is a bit out of date, I haven't rewritten it for thirty years
I've always been interested in this area of employment	All I really want is my old job back
I have an in-depth knowledge which could be transferred to a different area of employment, especially since there is an overlap of skills	I've worked in the same area of employment for thirty years, and don't know if I could change careers now
I have no objection to working for a woman. The age or sex of my boss or my work colleagues doesn't worry me	I would prefer not to work for a woman *or* I would find it difficult to work for anyone younger than me

I have a lot of work experience which, combined with my updated skills makes me a very useful member of any team	I've never needed to update my skills as they were perfectly suited to my old job
I'm willing to be flexible	I've always done it this way

Don't be put off or feel undermined if the person interviewing you is younger than you are. There isn't any reason to mention your age. If you are asked any questions that you feel are either too personal or not relevant to the job, maybe your interviewer is searching for your age, trying to find out if you are a carer or have family responsibilities. You should firmly but politely make it clear that it's the job opportunity that you have come to discuss and are eager to learn about, and that nothing else is relevant. Don't drop your guard and give away information about yourself that makes your age obvious. This can be easily done when you are led to believe the job is yours, or that the interview is over and your interviewer is making casual conversation and you have relaxed.

Make sure that you let your interviewer know that you base your decisions on commitment, sound judgement and your interpersonal skills. If you don't have all the right qualifications, then sell yourself on your experience, track record and employment stability. Of course, make it clear that you are always more than willing to go on any training courses that an employer offers to send you on. This shows that you have drive, an enquiring mind, an ability to absorb information and are forward thinking.

Bear in mind during your interview what employers are looking for when they are hiring older workers. Their criteria tend to be:

• ability and capability

• an alert and positive attitude

• energy and determination

• adaptability

• willingness to learn and change

- fit into the organisation

- knowledge

- experience – both work and life related

- balanced mature outlook.

SECOND SKILLS

Look back constructively on your work experience. You may have started your working life doing something totally different. During your career you may have developed a second skill, so now could be the time to bring that to the forefront.

THIS IS exactly what Shirley did when redundancy ended her thirty-year career as a television make-up artist. She had started her training at the BBC when she was eighteen and ended up as the head of a make-up department and make-up training school for one of the largest television companies in the UK. At fifty-one, with a redundancy pay off, she decided that although she was offered another job running another make-up department, she wanted to do something else.

'A couple of years before I was made redundant I realised I'd had enough. It wasn't fun any more and I was exhausted from working eighteen hour days. But I knew that when I left I didn't want to just sit around, so I started to think about what else I could do.' Shirley realised that for most of her career, one of the skills she had developed was learning to listen. 'When you're doing someone's make up, you're the last person they see before they go on and they're nervous, so they jabber away and you learn to listen – you don't get involved, just listen.'

Shirley realised listening was something she had become good at and enjoyed. She wondered how she could use this new skill. 'I decided to try training in one of the listening professions. I thought I might make a counsellor for Relate as I'd been married and divorced.'

Shirley trained with Relate for four years and is now a qualified counsellor; she is also three years into her psychotherapy training and has started to see her own clients. 'I now love what I do, it's so rewarding seeing people getting better.'

Shirley had assessed her skills, both those that she had been using to earn her living with for most of her working life, and those that she had 'collected' on the way. She decided that she didn't want to continue working in the same area, partly because it had changed significantly and also because she felt that as she was getting older she didn't have the energy and the enthusiasm. She recognised that during her working life she had collected various skills, one of them being 'listening'. She then found a way of positively transferring this skill from just being an unpaid daily social addition to her job, to something that was the basis for her to learn a whole range of new skills which she could then transfer to a new career. Shirley was not put off by her age and she used her redundancy pay off to cushion her while she moved towards a new form of employment. She chose a new career that not only suited her skills, but was totally different from anything she had ever done before, so she was able to move into it with new energy and enthusiasm. It also suited her age as it is a career that doesn't require physical strength. Shirley now has the freedom to continue working in her new career for as long as she wants.

Many outplacement consultants (people who find employment for those who want to work outside of the main workplace) say that they are seeing a lot of people who have been very successful, but as they get older they don't want to dance any longer to the organisation's tune. They want more control over what they do and when they do it. Many of their clients are in their mid-fifties and decide that they don't want to take on another executive job, but do non-executive directorships, consultancy assignments and charity work, which they have been unable to commit to before. They also want more time for their personal lives. You may find that consultancy, working in an advice centre, training or teaching are all areas that you are well suited for, bringing with you your years of experience and knowledge, plus your re-training to bring you up to date.

RE-TRAINING

Re-training is important as you get older because it widens your employment chances, and adds more strings to your bow, which could help you to make career changes. It shows that you are adaptable, and it will boost your self-esteem and confidence. A basic knowledge of the new technology counts; you'll find that it's generally user friendly and most adult education centres now offer IT training courses, which will give you a good grounding. This also gives you the opportunity to meet people who are in a similar position and of a similar age, so it gives you the opportunity to broaden your network. All of us, but especially once we reach our forties and early fifties, have to approach the new job market with flexibility, enthusiasm and an ability to sell our skills and services. As most of us are now living longer and staying healthier, we will soon be planning our employment in to the fourth age!

THE LEARNING AGE

Whatever your age you should remember that when it comes to employment, whether paid or unpaid:

• you have talents that should be allowed to grow and expand

• you are responsible for your life and work is part of life

• you should all find ways of discovering and developing your creative potential.

You should be encouraged by the fact that there are plenty of instances which show that age does not inhibit learning. For example 15 per cent of those studying for an MBA degree, one of the toughest business qualifications, are over forty. The Open University proves that some people in their eighties are capable of graduate level studies.

Despite the fact that people over fifty are excluded from student loans in higher education and have suffered from the closure of many adult education programmes, there are still a wide range of courses covering an assortment of subjects and interests. The University of the Third Age (U3A) is one of the largest organisations offering a self-help learning co-operative for older people, generally aged fifty plus. You don't have to have any qualifications to join and this particular university doesn't award any. Members meet and share interests, acquire new skills and expand their knowledge. Men and women with a lifetime of experience and expertise in a range of professions, occupations and hobbies form study groups and share their knowledge and their interests. They cover a wide range of subjects from 'Life in China' to 'PCs for Beginners'. There are over 300 U3As in the UK with a membership of 63,000. They are also to be found throughout Australia. The equivalent in the US, Canada and Bermuda is the Institute for Learning in Retirement (ILR). There are more than 250 ILRs affiliated to local colleges and universities offering those over fifty a wide range of subjects and interests.

CHAPTER 4

Role Reversal

The changing face of employment means that many women are now better equipped than ever before to cope with the modern world of work. Many are now taking on part-time and freelance positions and setting up in business. By contrast, many men are coming to terms with no longer having a job for life and are finding themselves at home looking after the family, a role that many of them are finding difficult.

WOMEN IN EMPLOYMENT

The story of the employment of women has been short and dramatic. At the beginning of the twentieth century only half of all thirty-year-old women, and less than a third of those with children, were employed. By the late 1940s and 1950s few women with children worked outside of the home. Many women of this generation described themselves in their passports as 'housewives'. It wasn't anything they were ashamed of, it wasn't politically incorrect and it didn't show they lacked ambition. They were simply fulfilling the role they had prepared for in school, encouraged by their families and learnt from their mothers, which was to look after their children, their husbands and their homes. If they ever had any ambitions of their own they were put firmly aside.

There have been huge changes for women in employment and

as we near the millennium the number of employed women in the UK is running almost neck and neck with employed men at more than 11 million, and 1.5 million of these women have a child under five (Office of National Statistics). Across the world, if unrecorded work done by women is taken into account – people who sew and knit and are paid in cash; grandmothers who care for grandchildren, freeing their daughters to be able to go out to work; farmers' wives who feed the chickens and muck out the pigs; housewives who care for their children and look after their homes – women do about 55 per cent of the world's work.

The recorded numbers of women working in industries and trades across Europe varies: in France 44 per cent of women are working; in Spain 35 per cent; in Italy 37 per cent; and in Germany and the UK 43 per cent. By the year 2000, 80 per cent of jobs worldwide are expected to go to women and by 2006 the number of working women is expected to rise by nearly 1 million, with almost three-quarters of the increase among those aged between thirty-five and fifty-nine.

So why is there this dramatic swing towards women working? Is it because women have finally gained equality in a man's world? Or is it, as is more likely, that the man's world is changing and because of recession, downsizing, outsourcing and a significant decline in male-dominated manufacturing industries, jobs have shifted to the service sector, an area where women have traditionally always found work. And, as the demand for manual labour continues to tail off and automation increases, the division of work where jobs were once defined as 'women's jobs and men's jobs', will not exist.

Women are also more likely than men to be single parents bringing up children, or to be elderly and living alone. There are a growing number of women who are relying on their own incomes for maintaining themselves and their families, and saving for when they are elderly. There are also a large number of women known as the 'sandwich generation', who delayed marriage in order to pursue their education and careers, had their children later and are now at a prime working age. These women are exhausted from caring for young children on the one hand and elderly parents on the other, while continuing to work.

Education and satisfactory additional child care are just two of the ways in which you can ensure that as a woman you are not left shouldering all of this increased burden. Education will help you to improve your chances of getting a higher paid job, while additional child care will relieve you of some of the exhaustion and stress. It is vital that women continue to break down barriers in the sciences and other professions, to move forward into managerial work and away from more traditional female areas of employment such as assembly lines, shop and catering trades. To achieve this women must continue into higher education, as the figures show: currently in the UK, only 8.2 per cent of women graduates are unemployed a year after they graduate, compared to 12.25 per cent of men. You must make sure that you are equipped with the necessary skills in order to keep pace with fast-moving technology and, like men, must now be capable of changing careers several times during your working life.

MOVERS AND SHAKERS

When it comes to women moving up in the world of power and decision making, progress is painfully slow. According to the US Fund for a Feminist Majority, it will be at least another 450 years before women are represented in equal numbers with men in the corridors of economic power. That's slow. Globally, fewer than 20 per cent of managers and 6 per cent or fewer of senior managers are women. At the current rate of progress women won't reach equality with men in decision making positions until the year 2465, and a United Nations study puts the date even further away, at the year 2490 ! We should also be aware that pay is actually falling for women, and the differences between what women and men are earning is growing wider.

According to the research none of us want to wait that long, and all the evidence shows that women are impatient and pushing and demanding, both individually and collectively to reach positions of power, not just concentrated in traditionally female areas of employment such as education and nursing, but in banking, management, joining the board and making decisions at executive level. In the US the situation is improving. Companies have a higher proportion of women managers, making important decisions, with eight women for every hundred men, compared to companies in Asia and Europe, where the ratio is one woman for every hundred male executives.

In the UK most women executives can be found at the lower end of corporate decision making, not in the boardroom, although there are obvious exceptions, such as the high profile Anita Roddick (founder of The Body Shop), Debbie Moore (founder of the Pineapple Dance Studios), and Steve Shirley (founder of the FI software group in the 1960s, who changed her name on her letter heading from Stephanie to Steve in order to get through the corporate door before anyone realised her gender – it worked!).

In Singapore the number of female managers has tripled in the last decade and a fifth of all businesses are owned by women. In Thailand the number of women managers increased five-fold between 1974 and 1990, while the number of male managers only doubled. In Japan nearly all the currency traders are women. In the seemingly unlikely settings of Togo and Ghana, the 'Mama Benz' women – so called because they own Mercedes Benz cars – are a powerful business group controlling much of the national cloth trade. They have counterparts in Zaire, Angola and other countries, and wield great influence over national and cross-boundary trade. The male dominant workforce is even being challenged in China, where one-third of the total of 14 million self-employed people are women.

And in the UK women are finally making inroads into the professions: 52 per cent of new solicitors; 32 per cent of managers and administrators; 34 per cent of health professionals; and 27 per cent of buyers, brokers and sales representatives are women. Worldwide the numbers of professional jobs are growing faster than any other occupational group and women are forecast to fill around 44 per cent of all these posts by 2001. Women are being employed in accountancy, law and medicine in equal numbers to men.

NEW WORK FORCE OR A FORCE TO BE RECKONED WITH?

Although women now number almost half of the workforce, are we an employment force to be reckoned with? Are we assertive enough to have a voice in the workplace that is heard? Certainly women who are under thirty are more likely than their mothers' generation to describe themselves as 'independent, assertive and competitive', and they are also more comfortable with being the centre of attention, characteristics which are traditionally perceived as leadership qualities displayed in men.

However, it is the case that many women still find being assertive difficult, especially at work. Indeed, I used to find it quite hard to make sure that my needs and opinions were heard, probably because assertive women were often described as being 'bossy, nagging, bitchy and hard'. I began to realise that when I wasn't being assertive my needs were not met and my opinions were not heard. This affected my career progress and prevented me from having the chance of moving on to a better, higher paid job, where I could have a say in what I did and the way in which I did it. I have always worked in male-dominated industries. At one advertising agency I was the only women working there apart from the receptionist. When I first joined the younger men made my working day very difficult with sexual innuendoes and being asked to do copywriting jobs that they didn't want to. That was until I became one of the 'boys', which I did by being friendly but as assertive as they were.

Dr Robert McHenry, a leading psychologist and chairman of Oxford Psychologists Press, told delegates at the Institute of Personnel Development that for the first time as many young women as young men describe themselves as being dominant. Only 15 per cent of 3,000 women recently surveyed defined themselves by their sex, and almost half felt that they were naturally superior. It's predicted that young women will become a force to be reckoned with in the workplace of the future because they are in the unique position of being able to combine skills from both traditional camps – the assertiveness of their fathers and the team instinct of their mothers.

If you have difficulty being assertive, Assertiveness Training Classes which are run by most local authorities as evening courses can be a positive help. Or try Cognitive Behaviour Training – a course of between twelve and sixteen sessions will help boost your self-esteem.

SKILLS FOR THE FUTURE

Both men and women agree that women are well equipped for the new world of work, with their talents for managing time, understanding other people's problems, giving good service to customers and adapting to changing methods of working. If you are a woman there is no reason why you shouldn't continue to sweep ahead in employment terms. Women have got it right and all future predictions show that this will continue.

In the new employment both part-time and service-based workers are in demand. The skills needed in these areas are:

- flexibility

- efficiency

- good service

- team work

- initiative.

And these are skills generally associated more with women than men. The only positive characteristic women apparently lack is the ability to organise others. Men still believe that they are better at this.

If you want to keep pace with the 'new skills', check what IT skills are needed for your area of employment, you may have to do this at least once a year to keep pace with the fast changing technology. Be prepared to pay for your own re-training.

PART-TIME WORK/SELF-EMPLOYMENT

Part-time work

Part-time work has always been seen as a career backwater, but for a million working women it's the work that suits them and often the only work they can find. Women make up 90 per cent of part-time workers in Germany and Belgium, 65 per cent in Italy, Greece and the US and 63 per cent in The Netherlands. This type of work is often badly paid and the chances of being trained or getting promoted are rare. The work involved tends to be at the lower end of the job market, such as cleaners, counter hands, shelf stackers and secretaries. Part-time work wouldn't ever pay enough to keep a family. Having said this the majority of part-time workers say that they are satisfied with their working hours, their jobs and the spare time it gives them. Many mothers make a positive choice to work part time in order to be with their children as much as possible.

In companies where part-time working has been offered, many employees have jumped at the opportunity. The Inland Revenue's agreement to allow its full-time employees with family commitments or other special circumstances to opt for part-time working has benefited more than 10 per cent of its workers in the last decade. When British Airways decided to 'downsize' by offering employees the option of shorter hours, with the same hourly wage, pension rights and other conditions, they had no shortage of volunteers. In fact the management not only met its targets for a smaller workforce, but saved on the cost of redundancy payments as well.

If you want to work part time but don't want to leave your present job, talk to your employer, you may be surprised how flexible they are willing to be, but be prepared, of course, for a drop in salary.

It is predicted that part-time employment will increase and not only in low-paid areas of work but also in the professions. Check out employers who are already willing to pay part-time workers the same rates as full-time employees.

'I don't want the job of oiling the wheels of someone else's dream'

Self-employment is becoming increasingly popular with women, allowing many of them to get round the difficulties of child care, and to shine in their own right. In the 1980s, according to the Department of Education and Employment, self-employment for women in the UK rose to 81 per cent compared to 51 per cent for men. Women are fast becoming the new small-scale entrepreneurs, finding satisfaction and success in starting up their own businesses. Self-employment has been empowering for women, giving them a work situation where they can advance their position and assert their equality.

NICKY, a twenty-seven-year-old photographic producer, is on the verge of joining the ranks of self-employed women who are running their own businesses. After leaving art college with a degree and a vague idea that she wanted to be a photographer she got a job as an assistant trainee PA in a large photographic studio and worked her way up to photographer's manager.

Three years down the line Nicky realised that she hated the world of fashion photography and decided to leave her job. 'I took a basic IT skills course, then I networked, sent out hundreds of CVs and did cold calling. But the only business I had contacts in was fashion photography and I didn't want to do that any more.'

After three months Nicky was still unemployed, but then she heard about a business idea. When her bike mechanic mentioned that he knew a guy who was opening a specialist motorbike shop in the city, Nicky realised this was what she wanted to be involved in, 'I couldn't sleep that night I was so excited. I had so many ideas.'

Nicky has gone into partnership with the originator of the idea and the two of them are about to buy premises. Nicky will be doing the marketing, managing the workshop and selling motorbikes. 'I've come from a women-run industry where women have control, to a male-run industry, and I think it's a massive advantage. The press will love the fact that I'm a woman. I don't want to work for anyone ever again. I don't want the job of oiling the wheels of someone else's dream.'

Nicky is not unusual, in Sweden and Finland more than a quarter of businesses are owned by women. In America, women-owned businesses now employ more people than the whole of the Fortune 500, with sales exceeding $1 billion, in forty-nine metropolitan districts. One-third of Australian small and medium sized businesses are owned or controlled by women. Even conservative estimates predict that women will run 40 per cent of small businesses in the UK by the end of the century. These small firms will thrive in the flatter, shifting, skills-based work structure predicted for 2010.

EDUCATION

If you have had a break from work or you want to change employment tracks, you may well find that the career you now want to pursue involves re-training and further education. My postman, for example has decided he wants a new career working in computers, but all the jobs he has applied for require at least basic English and maths at O level, on top of computer skills. He says he mucked around at school and left without any qualifications, so at thirty-six he's decided to go for it and two afternoons a week he's in an adult education classroom studying for his O levels, plus bringing his computer skills up to speed.

When you rejoin formal education it can take a while to get your brain back up to learning speed, as Jane another returner-learner discovered when she decided to take up a new career which required new qualifications.

JANE WAS a thirty-year-old secretary, who was laid off because the business was closing down. She looked around for more secretarial work, but she wasn't highly skilled and discovered that similar jobs to her old one were no longer available. Jane recalled that at school she had always wanted to be teacher. She had a particular love of geography, so Jane started at teacher training college to be a geography teacher. 'For the first three months I felt so stressed out because I was finding it so difficult to learn and I panicked that I wasn't going to be able to do it, whilst all the other students who were eighteen were finding it so easy because they'd just come out of school. It took me about a year to really get the hang of it and now I wish the college would give me more work. I loved teaching practice and I was much better at it than the 18 year olds, I think it's because I've had more life experience. I don't have any regrets about leaving school at eighteen and starting work, because looking back I know that I couldn't have gone straight to teacher training college from school, I just wasn't up to it, now I feel much more confident.' Jane has re-trained for a job with a future, and found fresh challenges in her new career.

If you are an education returner like Jane there are now over 250 universities or colleges offering 42,000 different courses in cities or campus sites around the UK, which give you a greater subject choice than ever before. Anyone can apply, regardless of your age, background or even academic history as most colleges and universities now offer access courses in case you don't have the required qualifications.

When you return to college you'll find that younger students tend not to be as bothered about your age as perhaps you are. Your additional life experiences will give you extra confidence and working knowledge and the enthusiasm of younger people can be very energising. Going back to college, either full or part time is a positive way of re-training for a new career and you'll find that additional qualifications can be a big boost to your self-confidence in the world of work. Certainly if you are thinking about joining the professions, which include accountancy, the law, medicine, architecture, teaching and many others, you could either return to college full time or continue your present job whilst getting the necessary qualifications on a part time basis or through distance learning or evening classes. You may find that you are able to use your old qualifications that you got years ago and bring them up to date with additional training – this is possible in employment areas such as nursing, teaching and accountancy.

The next generation of women are already better educated

than their mothers and when you educate a woman you educate a family. We know that women invest proportionately more in the health and education of their children than men do, and research shows that educated mothers are better able to prepare their children for school and later on when they need to earn a living. It is the mother's education, rather than the father's, which has a strong influence on the educational and occupational aspirations of daughters, plus education gives women the opportunity to learn about their legal rights and have the necessary self-confidence to use those rights. Even on a basic level, education makes it possible to check your wages accurately, make sure that you are getting the correct benefits and to report and take action against sexual harassment and discrimination in the workplace.

If you are thinking of studying for a degree as a mature student, don't just pick a subject that you think you'll be good at, make sure that in some way it matches your career ambitions, the two may not always be obvious. Before making your choice check it out with a careers analyst or the adult careers guidance person at the college of your choice. If you have a family or a partner you should involve them in your decision to return to learning as you are about to become a hard-working student with the additional pressure of homework and a fixed timetable.

Even though you may want your career to take a more executive direction, don't overlook skills, which although they may be outside of your business qualifications, will help you to deal with colleagues, show that you understand the new technology and understand the workings of business management. Courses in the following subjects will be helpful and look good on your CV, giving you an edge over your competitors:

- business management

- decision making

- assertiveness

- people skills

- IT skills

- team work

- communication skills.

Many of these courses are available through your local adult education authority and there are a number of employers who provide training. Although you may not think the training you are offered is relevant to your job or what you want to do in the future, you'll be surprised how many skills are transferable. If changing jobs is the only way for you to move up the corporate ladder you must be prepared to fund your own training. You should also consult a head hunter from within your particular industry.

Child Care

The education and energy that career changes and employment require are doubly difficult for women to achieve because many of them are also carers. In some families where parents are either self-employed, part-time workers or job sharers, they are able to share their child care. Others who work or study at set times are left to rely on grandparents, relatives or neighbours to take over the role of carer.

Your children can be cared for at home by a nanny, who will have a professional qualification, but this can be very expensive. Au pairs are a cheaper option, but always use a reputable agency and check references and check that the agency has checked the references. Alternatively your child can be placed in a day care centre or a local nursery but demand often outstrips supply. Crèche facilities are now being offered by some adult education colleges and some employers.

Some local authorities have lists of registered childminders in their area. This system isn't a fool-proof method of vetting carers, but it can give you some reassurance and you will know that the child-minder's house has been inspected for cleanliness and safety. Local authorities also have lists of standard charges. Schools and nurseries also keep names of reliable childminders and will be able to put you in touch with them and with other parents who have previously used their services, which gives you a reference source.

REAL MEN EARN REAL MONEY – OR DO THEY?

In the new, more flexible workplace the labelling of jobs into categories, 'men's and women's', has almost disappeared and men will have to shed masculine stereotypes or lose out to women at work.

Some men continue to see their role as that of 'breadwinner', with expectations of pay that are no longer realistic, while women are often prepared to be more flexible and work for less money, which isn't progressive either. It's predicted that this employment scenario will change in the future as the old, male dominated work structure ceases to exist.

The traditional roles of men and women have broken down and women in many families are now the main earners, while the men are becoming more domesticated and taking responsibility for children and elderly relatives.

Practical Response and Emotional Support

Men are having to adapt to the new ways of working. Being employed part time or sharing a job can give you time with your family, ease the burdens of employment from your partner and enable you to bolster the family's earnings.

You may find that the area of work that you were employed in before no longer exists and you will have to take stock of your skills and your talents, probably re-train, and look for employment in areas that you might previously have considered unsuitable. This is what David had to do.

D AVID WAS a garage mechanic; his working life had always been oily rags and lying underneath cars. When the garage closed and he was made redundant, he went out looking for a new job. He discovered that most of the local garages had closed down, and those that survived had queues of people, all younger than David, wanting to work for them. He realised that he wasn't able to get a job working in the same area. As his redundancy money dwindled away, he had to sell his house and he and his wife – his children were all married – moved into a mobile home.

David became depressed, believing that he had failed his family and that he no longer felt he was a man. His wife found a job helping out in a local children's home, while David sat at home feeling that if he couldn't any longer be a garage mechanic, what could he do? Driven by debt, he finally took a job stacking shelves in his local supermarket. He mostly worked nights because the hourly rate was higher, while his wife worked days, and they passed each other in the bedroom at dawn. After a year the supermarket offered David a management training course. He took it, and a year later he is now one of the supermarket managers. His wife is training as a social worker, and they have bought a house and are about to have a holiday. David feels as if he has a new life. He says that he doesn't miss the oily rag one bit.

David is carving out a new career for himself. It may not have been in an area of employment he would ever have considered before, but like the majority of us when he was put in a no choice situation, he took the job opportunity that was on offer and turned it around to his advantage. Be positive. Only look back to take the positives out of the past. Research new areas of employment. Be prepared to work part time or any other job variation you may be offered. You aren't just looking for a job, you are looking for a new way of working.

MAIN EARNER BEHAVIOUR

If you were once the main earner, and are no longer, you and your partner need to ensure that you are supporting one another. Ask your partner to remember the following:

- By being at home you are working and contributing to the family.

- You are making a huge financial contribution by looking after the home and often the children as well. Reliable and loving child care is costly and difficult to find; cleaners can also be expensive.

- Decisions, especially about finances should continue to be made jointly.

- You are part of a team, and while some members of the team work outside of the home, others work inside.

- Your time at home is as exhausting as the main earner's time at the office – be considerate.

- It is important to share your leisure time with your family.

- You would appreciate encouragement as you look for employment, even if it isn't full-time employment.

- Feedback on your ideas and the research you've done looking for job opportunities is always welcome.

- You need encouragement to re-train.

- You may need your partner's help to do a DIY skills audit.

If you are a man who is a home carer you should try to:

- have another interest or hobby outside of the home such as a sport, part-time or voluntary work, part-time education, distance learning, helping around the neighbourhood, re-training, updating your IT skills

- be positive about your situation, see it as a stop-gap, giving you a chance to set out a new plan of action

- keep up to date with either the area of work that you were in or one that you want to move into by reading relevant trade journals and magazines, going to trade union meetings or keeping in touch with work colleagues

- make use of your local Job Club and Employment Office, both for careers advice and the facilities they offer, such as free use of computers and trade directories

- not to look back – the future is where your energy lies.

SEXUAL DISCRIMINATION

Sex discrimination in job advertisements or in the workplace is illegal. However, women can still find that they have to deal with 'male power', simply because more organisations are run by men than women and more men hold key positions.

So, if you work in a male-dominated area of employment and think:

• you are being sexually harassed

• you are having to deal with offensive male behaviour or male prejudices

• that your career opportunities are blocked because of your sex

then you should contact the Equal Opportunities Commission, your trade union or any other trade organisation that represents your particular area of employment.

Complaints about sexual discrimination towards men have increased by 50 per cent in the UK, according to the Equal Opportunities Commission. A survey by Reed Personnel Services showed that one in nine (11.9 per cent) of the total sample of 494 companies surveyed, have come across prejudice against employing men in secretarial jobs. This could be why the number of male secretaries is very small, estimated at just under 1 per cent, despite the fact that the number of men looking for secretarial work is increasing. Again, if you feel you have been discriminated against in such a way contact the Equal Opportunities Commission for advice.

THE PINK GHETTO

The pay gap between working men and women, known as the pink ghetto, can be found in almost every country in the world, regardless of how much progress has been made by women in other areas of employment. In France women make up half of all public servants, but they earn 19 per cent less than men since they are mostly employed in lower level jobs. In Japan most women work in small companies with few benefits, and in both the US and Russia, which you would think are unlikely employment partners, women make up 95 per cent of all the secretaries, 94 per cent of the cashiers and 80 per cent of the shop assistants. Although 40 per cent of Russian women are scientists and academics they make up only 2 per cent of the Soviet Academy of Sciences.

In 1998 women in the UK earned an average of just two-thirds of men's wages and were often, through either lack of qualifications, background education, child care responsibilities or finance, denied access to opportunities and education that would lead to a better job. When men and women do the same job, men's average earnings are nearly always higher. The pay gap is even wider for managerial jobs, such as bank and building society managers, than it is in professional occupations such as medical practitioners.

Some experts believe that in the new employment climate these pay differences will gradually change, as more flexible working patterns gain acceptance and more professional jobs can be done part time. For example, 80 per cent of employers in the UK believe that part-time working for managers will become increasingly popular in the future.

While there is no doubt that there are women able to provide and contribute towards their family earnings, many remain poorly paid. The average pay gap between men and women is still running roughly at around 20 per cent. The UK's Equal Opportunities Commission predicts that if the slow trend in achieving equal pay for women continues as it has over the last twenty years, it will be another forty-five years before women finally achieve equal pay with men. Armed with education and the correct qualifications, women must work towards equal pay in a shorter time than is being predicted. The way to help with this is to:

• join a pressure group

• report any pay gap to your trade union and the Equal Opportunities Commission

• make your personnel manager aware of any discrepancies.

CONCLUSION

There was a time when we separated our home life and our working life, but with flexible working, role reversal in families, redundancies and an ageing workforce, we can see this is no longer possible. This is why being adaptable and flexible, both at home and at work is the key to surviving in the new world of employment. If you are coming to terms with role reversal, you have to realise that you are both working for the family firm, both trying to achieve the same ends and that your joint aim is to support one another, not just financially but sharing both the stress and the responsibilities.

The individual benefits from role reversal can be enormous; if you are a woman it is a chance for you to flex your employment muscle, become self-confident and self-assured, get some on-the-job training and forge a career. Even if later on it has to go under wraps for a few years, you can always bring it up to date later. For men who find themselves at home, your support for your partner is vital. Being the main carer will also change your relationship with your children which is invaluable to the development of both of you, now and in the future. This can also be an opportunity to do a self skills audit, catch up on the new technology, re-train for a different future or a more interesting hobby and start a portfolio career. Your kick-off point could be networking the playground or the shared school run and making new friendships that might grow into working partnerships.

The workforce is ageing. Soon organisations will have to employ older workers because there will be fewer younger ones coming onto the job market. Life experience will be an employment bonus in a lot of areas. The new technology, from the laptop to the robot means that we aren't any longer required for our physical strength, which is what we lose with age. Instead, it will be our ability to master the new technology, to have enthusiasm and a willingness to adapt, to re-train and our range of skills which will be the future employment bonuses. As you get older part-time work, which was an employment backwater in the past, but is now being promoted as the fast lane of the future, begins to look very attractive. You don't have to run with the rats in the race any more, now you can cruise. In the changing world of work always look for the positive alternatives, not the negative dead ends.

PART 2

New Work

CHAPTER 5

New Workspace

Imagine working in a place:

- where your office telephone calls are replaced by a visual representation on a flat screen

- where you can talk to your office walls and they will pass on your messages

- where your wrist watch will give you verbal reminders, not your PA

- where you'll be able to join an out-of-town meeting, see everyone and participate, simply by putting on a pair of glasses

- where city traders will don headsets and trading will be done by virtual reality

- where video conferencing will be a stand-up event

- where groups meet in hologram form through a set of pre-arranged co-ordinates.

You may be surprised to know that this isn't science fiction; all of these things are already possible. In this chapter we will take a look at what you can expect to find in the new workspace.

Meetings taking place in smoke-filled boardrooms are already almost a thing of the past. The virtual meeting is with us, as the head of a large multinational company recently experienced when he was asked to chair a discussion on global technology issues. He wanted to know where this would take place and was told the meeting would be a virtual one. The delegates would be present via their desk-top, using the Internet to bring everyone together in a cyber form. Eat your heart out, corporate travellers, this could see an end to all those Air Miles, hotel perks, airport gifts, business class travel and expense accounts.

During the last fifty years we have slowly broken away from the stereotypes of the typing pool; segregated management areas; whole departments that never met, let alone interacted; and the hierarchy system, where the size and privacy of your office space advertised your power and importance within your organisation.

And look how far we've come. Thanks to the cellular phone, the lap-top and the modem you can work on trains, in airport lounges, hotel rooms or out of your car and you can telework from home before and after the school run. What previously desk-bound workers have discovered is that they don't any longer need to work behind a desk all the time – and sales people in particular have even less use for a permanent office space. Instead people are learning to use a kart – a filing cabinet on wheels – or a drawer, and hot desking or sharing office space to ensure that office resources are used more efficiently, such as in twenty-four-hour banking which consists of shift work, so the space we have, we learn to share.

For example, the chief executive of British Airways, one of the largest multinational corporations, realised that he couldn't recall when he had last spent more than five minutes behind his desk, so he decided to scrap it: 'The desk has gone and the space will be smaller and I will have a place to talk and listen to people without the formality of a conventional office.'

This way of working is now becoming more popular. In the most innovative firms in Britain, the US and Europe four walls and a desk are out. Employees now enjoy 'clubbing', 'quiet rooms', 'lagoons' and 'breaking out'. It may all sound like gobble-de-gook to some of you now, but this is the language of the new workplace.

Many organisations have already dramatically changed their

working environment, from the layout of the office to the lack of status symbols. In order to thrive and survive in the new workplace you have got to be prepared to change and understand the new terminology. Here are a few definitions of new office words:

- **lagoon**   a group of people working at desks facing outwards
- **breaking out**   a place for casual chat
- **hot desking**   sharing desk space
- **small desk**   for short-term working
- **work stations**   for long-term working
- **quiet rooms**   for decision making or private conversation
- **cockpit**   a small, enclosed, individual room.

You will find a more comprehensive list of the new jargon in Part 4 of this book.

In the new workplace, don't expect:

- partitioned offices and your own desk
- rigid office boundaries supporting the hierarchy system
- filing cabinets – you now have a trolley on wheels with your work in it.

WORKING IN THE NEW WORKPLACES

There are already a few workplaces where territory and job status no longer equal large desk and your own office door. Gone are the rigid boundaries, power offices, whole floors designated executive-only areas, with the executive washroom and an executive-only restaurant. Now staff hop from desk to desk and from free space to bean bag. One person who works in this kind of office environment admitted that it took her some time to get used to it, 'I had previously had my own large office, a marble desk, pictures of my own choice on the walls and my own favourite plants and comfy chair. I found it pretty hard to get used to going from that to sitting next to someone new every day.'

One of the top UK accountancy companies, not an area of employment normally known for being innovative, has moved into the new century with its workspace by dividing office areas into sections for six groups of two hundred, each with large workstations for long-term work, small desks for short-term work and airport lounge style space for conversational work. Meeting rooms have been made larger, some with sofas and table lamps to make them more homely – these rooms are very popular and are often fully booked. Actually having to work in the new work space on a daily basis has its fors and againsts as Mary discovered when the organisation she works for dramatically changed their office working environment.

MARY IS A senior manager at a large consultancy firm. Although she is in a senior position she works in a large, open-plan office with a hundred other employees all from different grades within the company. 'I think open plan helps with the integration of staff,' she says. 'As a senior manager I'm out there with everyone else, I'm more accessible, staff can just walk up to my desk any time they want. I think they like being able to do that and so do I. Although obviously I don't hear everything that's going on, the partners in the company expect us to keep our ears to the ground and pick up any problems, and I've certainly learnt, since working in an open-plan area, to sense when there's an atmosphere. I also think that all of us being together helps people to bond better and makes for a friendlier working atmosphere. The down side is that when I'm working with confidential papers, such as when I'm involved in a staff appraisal, I don't have any privacy. Of course I can go and book a "hot office", but if I don't, then I have to clear my desk and put everything in my drawers every time I even go to the loo.'

Mary enjoys some aspects of her new work space and can see the advantages both to the organisation and to the other employees, but like anything new there are parts of it that she finds tedious and will have to devise her own system for working in. But overall the pluses outweigh the minuses.

Being aware that some people find working in the new open environment stressful, organisations often interview an applicant five or six times for any job, be it creative or a receptionist, because they know that it takes a certain type of person to feel happy working in this way.

In order to survive in this type of workspace you must be flexible and not expect to be surrounded by the same setting, such as your own desk and filing cabinet. See the positive advantages of a more open environment Get rid of all the garbage in your working life such as the family photographs, the desk drawers full of bent paper clips and broken elastic bands. Only have what you need to work with, the tools of your trade. Learning to ignore exterior conversation and noise may not be easy at first if you have been used to having your own private workspace, but you will find that most people respect others' need for silence. People realise that just being able to walk over to someone and discuss ideas makes them more easily accessible, but that it is important to become sensitive to their concentration levels and work rhythms, and allow them to become sensitive to yours.

Of course, progress is slow and a lot of the changes in our working environment are only very gradually taking place. So public zones exist for meetings, and open-plan offices are already commonplace; managers have offices with glass walls for accessibility, but blinds to give them privacy when necessary. What is important is that you are prepared for the office of the future and able to adapt to the new working environments.

More Computers – Fewer People

As a result of downsizing those middle managers who are left behind now find themselves being asked to do more with less. The computer has replaced secretaries, PAs and general office brain storming, so there is little need for walls and divisions. Conversations between computers are silent and therefore private and can take place anywhere. One computer hardware manufacturer reports that in the very near future everything that is now carried by cables, will go through the airwaves and that leads and wiring tangled across floors and up walls will be replaced by infra-red signals connecting computers to servers, communication networks and the Internet, and that those confrontational desks and chairs will be replaced by creative virtuality zones.

Most organisations are certainly aware of the mobility of machines and are moving away from chunky PCs to more slimline lap-tops, which enable staff to 'plug and play'.

In the new workplace, you should be prepared to:

- do your work with a computer not a colleague

- learn everything possible about the technology you are expected to work with

- not rely on having a secretary, since you will be expected to write your own business letters and memos, so learn to do it well and efficiently

- become organised, as you will be expected to keep your own diary, make your own appointments and do your own time-keeping – self-sufficiency is the name of the game

- understand how your computer and the Internet can cut your workload if you know how to use them correctly. Be prepared to fund your own IT course every few years, in order to stay ahead of the technology game.

The Great Paper Chase

Despite the huge advances in new technology and the way that the computer and the Internet now dominate the majority of our working lives, our biggest work comforter continues to be paper and we are clinging on to it rather like our status symbol private offices and large desks. No book about the future of work would be complete without acknowledging that we have to learn to live without so much paper if we are to survive in the working world of the new technology.

As a writer and a journalist I am a major consumer of paper, even though I dislike the litter of it all over my desk, and the way even more of it chugs out of my fax, printer and photocopier. My stationery cupboard bulges with reams of it and daily more of it crashes though my letterbox. But I am finding I am able to use paper less and less, as I store thousands and thousands of pages on my computer, which don't get torn or fade and are easily accessible. I can compose a letter on the screen and send it via e-mail, and even internal office memos can now be sent around the office via the internal Intranet. You can have your own personal fax number that is routed to your own e-mail system wherever you are in the world. You will also be able to transfer voice-mail into readable text. In the new workplace paper does not have such an important place and we must learn to transfer our communication skills to the new technology.

WHO NEEDS AN OFFICE?

The idea of the office becoming obsolete is something I find very exciting. It's actually possible because the new technology is so mobile that where we actually do our work begins to be unimportant. If the last ten years have been about re-engineering the factory floor to compete in a global marketplace, then the next ten are going to be about the building-less office.

Many companies have already armed their staff with mobile phones, lap-tops, fax cards and home business lines. They have introduced sophisticated telephone systems which enable calls to be re-routed to staff wherever they are. The corporate office block, in the words of one digital guru, will eventually become 'more of a utility building'. The imposing office towers will in effect end up being large, imposing customer centres. Although companies still prefer to have headquarters, what will change is how that space is used.

If technological mobility means that we can now work anywhere, why not from home? Experts in this field are forecasting that 50 per cent of jobs in London could be done, at least in part, by wired-up outworkers using computers. Some figures show that 15 per cent of the total salaried British workforce is already working at home This isn't surprising considering that the rewards for employers are lower costs and higher productivity, and for employees technology has made homeworking simplicity in itself. The trend can only accelerate.

This doesn't mean that if you choose to work from home you have to have a filing cabinet in your hall and an office-sized photocopier in your children's playroom. The basic needs of a homeworker are now so compact and simple, all you will need are a telephone (and perhaps a mobile phone), fax, modem, PC and printer, and all of these are decreasing in size, cost and ugliness. The central element of working at home will be the computer, and the faster and the more powerful it is the better. This will take you into the next millennium and the guesstimate is that by then homeworkers will have holographic storage – this is terabyte technology which is the equivalent of 1,000,000,000,000 bytes (units of computer data), that can three-dimensionally store the contents of a video library in the space of a sugar cube.

A new bandwidth mobile-phone network is under development, which will provide services such as portable video calls and even the ability to dial up a favourite movie that you will be able to watch on your handset screen. As for size, there is already a mobile phone that weighs less than 100g, and is so small that it can be worn as a pendant which discreetly vibrates rather than rings to let you know when you have a call.

Computers

According to Professor Peter Cochrane, Head of Advanced Applications and Technologies at British Telecom, within the next decade you can expect to be working with computers one thousand times more powerful than those you work with today, growing to over one million times more powerful within the next twenty-five years. These will become a key feature of your future working environments, as will talking to machines, communicating face-to-face and information on demand. Technology is changing fast and so are the costs. There isn't any need to continually up grade, however much pressure sales people put on you. There are times when as the saying goes, 'if it ain't broke, don't mend it'.

E-mail

E-mail is a vital tool for the new workspace because it can be used to replace the office memo, to contact clients anywhere in the world and even to transfer, as electronic attachments, entire files – words or pictures – from PC to PC. Some also have a dial-in facility to a fax machine which can deliver e-mail.

ISDN

The main touchstone of teleworking is the ability to connect remote PCs either to each other or to a central database to allow the exchange of data such as messages and files. This Integrated Services Digital Network (ISDN) makes the process of communication very much faster. It allows the transmission of voice, data, fax and video digitally, via an ordinary telephone line, at speeds far in excess of those possible over a standard telephone, three hundred times faster than anything that can be achieved by the fastest modem. It is compatible throughout the world and in some countries it's free, but in the UK it remains an expensive form of communication as there is a charge for installation, a monthly standing charge, plus phone charges.

ENJOY IT!

The new workplace is a very different world, from its very structure to the ways in which you will interact with your work colleagues. Technology allows you to be more mobile so that you will no longer require a desk or a permanent office, and you can work just as easily sitting in your car as you can in a plane. If you decide to work from home you no longer need to clutter the place with large, ugly pieces of office equipment; you can have up-to-the minute communication and processing power with just a few small pieces of high-powered technology. It's very exciting. The work is changing and so is the face of it and the ways in which you do it. You now have to adapt and let go of the old ways of working and enjoy the freedom and versatility that technology is able to bring you.

To adapt to a new working environment, remember, more high tech, less stagnant and hierarchical. Don't get bogged down in office status symbols. If you are setting up your own office choose small, high-powered equipment. Research the technology to match your needs and shop around. Enjoy the movement, space and interaction that technology allows you.

CHAPTER 6

Alternative Ways of Working

As we reach the millennium, flexible is the 'F' word in employment. All sorts of jobs ranging from management to shop-floor work, from professional to casual, can now be done in a flexible way to suit your lifestyle and out-of-work commitments. Don't rush into a way of working that you may find in the long term does not suit your family or financial requirements and is a career backwater. This chapter will help you to examine your options before making your choice.

PART-TIME WORK

According to a Labour Force Survey the number of part-time workers in the UK has almost doubled to 6.5 million, that's around a quarter of the workforce. and 80 per cent of these are women. In the finance sector, where part-time work is growing rapidly, because a lot of transactions are now done over the phone from call centres or by a computer, the figure is expected to reach 43 per cent by the year 2001.

Part-time workers are usually defined as those who work fewer than the normal hours of a comparable full-time worker. Government statistics define a part-time worker as someone who works fewer than thirty hours a week, although many people who work more than that define themselves as working part time. Full-time hours tend to be between thirty-eight to forty hours a week, although many employees work far more hours than that especially in this climate of employment fear (see Chapter 10).

A recent survey by the Institute of Employment Research, shows that by the year 2000 one in three of those of us who are working will be employed part-time. You may find that the company that you work for is keen on taking you on a part-time basis. This is because many organisations are becoming more flexible with their employment arrangements and have discovered the advantages to both the employer and those that they employ. If you are finding it difficult to get full time employment then you will probably find that part-time work is easier to get and the advantage is that the flexibility that it offers allows you time to do other things of your choice.

PAUL WAS made redundant at about the time that his first child was born. Both he and his partner decided they wanted to spend as much time as possible with their new son, and both chose to work part time. They were both offered jobs where they could work between twenty-six and thirty hours a week. They thought about working 'back to back' (one doing a day job and one of them working evenings) but then realised that they wouldn't ever see each other. Their solution was to both work half a day, crossing over at lunchtime when a child minder looked after their son. They feel they have gained a lot out of part-time working, as it has allowed each of them to spend more time with their child than if they had been working full time.

Pros And Cons

Part-time work allows you the freedom to use your non-working time to do what you want: be with your children; take up adult education; earn some income while pursuing a creative activity that you enjoy.

Traditionally part-time work has been low skilled, poorly paid and often insecure. Six out of ten part-time workers in Britain do not get the same contractual rights as their full-time counterparts, such as paid holidays, sick leave, occupational pensions, staff discounts and share options. However, recently there has been significant improvement in the terms and conditions offered to part-time workers, for example in the last few years some employers have extended their pension schemes to cover part-time employees.

Skills And Resources

You will need to be:

- adaptable

- flexible

- able to use a keyboard

- skilled with people, especially necessary for retail work

- able to 'fit in' and learn quickly.

Part-Time Jobs

There are a whole range of jobs that have proved to be very suitable for work on a part-time basis, including a small number at managerial level. For example the Chartered Institute of Management Accountants found in their survey of over a hundred companies that 73 per cent had some managers working part time. Part-time work is popular in areas of employment covering twenty-four hours, such as banking, supermarkets and fast food chains. Plenty of painters, sculptors, crafts people and writers use part-time work as a way of supplementing their income.

JOB SHARING

Job sharing started in the 1980s, pioneered by local authorities who offered full job share schemes to their employees. More recently the larger private companies have taken up the idea. In a 1995 Labour Market Survey 0.7 per cent of employees in the UK were working on a job sharing basis – 1.2 per cent of women and 0.2 per cent of men. Australian Government Statistics show that for men part-time work has doubled in the last ten years, but for women it has only increased by 29 per cent.

The basic idea behind job sharing is shared responsibility: this is where two people share the responsibility for one full-time job. Their duties aren't divided, the two of them are both able to perform the range of tasks required within that single job, meaning that one can pick up the job where the other has left off. Job sharing is becoming more popular and is now being offered across a wide range of employment, from teachers and solicitors, to administrators and nurses. Some of the employers who are offering job sharing at all levels include Marks & Spencer, Rover Group, most of the major high street banks, Shell, PowerGen PLC, Abbey National and Boots PLC.

Pros And Cons

The Industrial Society has concluded that not only does job sharing work, but that it has proved a positive success both for the organisations and the job sharers. The benefits most frequently mentioned by employers are as follows:

- Two people bring two sets of skills and experience to the job.

- People working reduced hours tend to be fresh, energetic and creative.

- They can also bring increased flexibility. For instance working peak periods together brings continuity and if one person is sick or on holiday at least part of the job gets done.

- It can make it easier for women wanting to return to work after maternity leave, if part-time work is unavailable.

- Men can work part time and spend more time with their children.

However, on the down side:

- it often doesn't pay well

- it can affect your promotion

- it can be difficult finding someone to share with.

A number of professional bodies or trade unions have registers which aim to match potential partners. Alternatively, some people advertise for a partner in a professional journal, local or trade union newspaper. Ask around your friends or work colleagues from a previous full-time job, who may now be interested in job sharing.

Your pension will be paid pro rata to your earnings, and you will be allowed exactly the same holiday leave as full-time employees, except you will be paid at the same rate that you would be getting if you were working.

Skills And Resources

You will need to be:

- flexible

- able to work closely with others

- able to share responsibility

- able to share ideas.

Job-Share Jobs

Jobs that are shared at all levels include GPs, hospital consultants, nurses, ward managers, probation officers, social workers, architects and planners, teachers, lecturers, personnel officers, journalists, solicitors, secretaries, administrators and police officers.

SELF-EMPLOYMENT

In 1996 self-employment accounted for 13 per cent of all employment. By 2006 this is expected to have risen to over 15 per cent. Self-employment for women has increased from 21 per cent of the total in 1981 to 25 per cent in 1996.

Being self-employed can free you from all the boundaries of regular full-time employment, but you should take into account not only the financial ups and downs, but also whether or not you have the ability to be a 'one person band'. You will also have the added responsibility of having to do everything connected with your business, even if you have the support of an understanding bank manager and a good accountant, two vital ingredients for success. You also have to be able to raise capital, understand a business plan, keep your accounts, be strong on self-marketing, promotion, selling, organisation, dealing with cash flow, be aware of any legal regulations connected with your product or service, plus the rules about becoming an employer yourself, as well as producing a product that will sell. It can be exhausting, especially if you are building a business from scratch.

Above everything self-motivation is vital. You have to have the self-motivation to get things done and this has to come from within you because there isn't a boss telling you what to do, when to do it and how to do it, the only person driving you forward is yourself (and your bank!). You'll find that self-motivation comes easier if you're doing something that you love, that interests you and to which you are committed. Dedication is the name of the game, with an exceptional dollop of energy. But, however much energy and dedication you have, to be successful you also have to have a good business idea.

SELF-EMPLOYED people also have a different interpretation of the word 'success', as author of *Go It Alone*, Geoff Burch, discovered when he walked out of his top corporate job and claims that he's never looked back. He chose to become self-employed, which he says has given him a type of freedom, 'I'm not necessarily talking about "free man" hippie type freedom, but a type of business freedom which allows you to be frighteningly efficient.' Despite this, Burch hit a low point and was finding every month a financial battle, until one day he met a respected business colleague, who introduced him to someone as 'a successful businessman'.

'Afterwards I got this friend on his own and asked him where he got the successful bit from,' says Burch, 'and he asked me how long I had been in business. I told him it was about four years and he replied, "And you're still here! I call that successful." '

Burch says that 'Fulfilment comes in different ways. Success can be as little as paying the bills and having a modest holiday now and again.'

If you decide to go down the self-employed route, remember that either you and/or your accountant will have to complete your Self-Assessment Tax Forms at the end of every tax year. There are financial advantages and disadvantages to being self-employed and your accountant or your local tax office will have a list of what businesses expenses are tax deductible. Don't forget your National Insurance payments and pensions. There will also be additional paperwork such as sending out invoices and making sure you are paid for the work you have done, and continuing to drum up new business, finding new clients either by word-of-mouth, or advertising in trade journals, local papers and free magazines. To some people this kind of hands-on work is exhilarating, whilst to others it's just plain tedious and time consuming, and all they want to do is get on with the job. Research the ins and outs of self-employment before you start; you'll find that there's plenty of useful information about. If you have friends who are self-employed ask them if you can pick their brains, most people find that type of question flattering and will be only too happy to help, and you'll find they can be a useful source of basic information.

Pros And Cons

The pros of self-employment are:

- it's perfect employment for entrepreneurs

- many business expenses are tax deductible

- it gives you a feeling of having more control over your working life.

While the cons are:

- there's no guarantee of a pay cheque at the end of every month

- you have to be prepared to take on the additional responsibility of doing everything connected with your business

- you have to be prepared to work unsociable hours

- there's a high burn-out rate – there's no such thing as a regular paid holiday any more.

Skills And Resources

Being self-employed requires a variety of skills including:

- self-motivation

- dedication

- energy

- good business sense

- self-marketing

- promotion

- selling

- organisation.

Many local authorities run business courses which will help you with bookkeeping, accounting, selling and marketing, and can give you information on the rules which govern specific types of businesses. More importantly they will give you advice on the sort of self-employed work that would suit someone with your interests, skills and employment background. They will also give you information on the training and the qualifications required. These sorts of courses automatically widen your network of contacts and help you meet people. Who knows, you may meet someone in the same area of business or training with the same interests and decide to go into business together.

You may prefer to have more than one field of self-employment, as separate amounts of money add up. This is how plumbers and electricians have always worked, so why not fashion consultants and personnel managers, for example?

Self-Employment Jobs

Just about anything and everything fits into self-employment, except assembly line work.

STARTING UP A SMALL BUSINESS

Starting up a small business seems to be especially appealing to women because it allows them to pick and choose the hours they work and gives them entrepreneurial freedom – something that many women have been denied in male dominated organisations. Because women are especially good at networking and organisation they are well suited to running a small business. Statistically almost every employment projection for Britain suggests that because of a decline in manufacturing, the impact of IT and the growth of the service sector, the economy will be dominated by small businesses. Women are powering the growth in this area with more than half of all business start-ups now in their hands. Because of their experience of under-promotion working in large organisations women running their own small business tend to manage their staff differently, being more likely to empower them, delegate and use supportive leadership which encourages open communication.

Meanwhile in the US statistics show that more businesses started by women fail; for example, 7 to 11 per cent more businesses started by women go to the wall than those started by men. But this failure isn't the result of bad management, lack of business knowledge or skills, it's more likely to be because women don't have access to capital. Despite women having greater career opportunities the majority of banks still tend to take women less seriously financially, and still prefer them to be backed by a man or have a male business partner. If you are involving your bank in your small business be prepared for them to want to see a detailed business plan showing that you have researched your specific section of the market, looked at the competition and costed your product competitively, while covering your overheads and allowing a profit margin.

Pros And Cons

The pros of setting up a small business are:

- it can give you a huge amount of job satisfaction and be very challenging

- it suits entrepreneurs

- it allows you make your own business decisions

- it's ideal for good networkers.

While the cons are:

- it can be hard work and involve long, unsociable hours

- the rewards can be slow in coming.

Skills And Resources

If you are thinking of starting your own business you should look at the following skills and resources.

- Do a business course: many are run by local education authorities; many private business schools run them, but these aren't cheap. You will find them advertised in business sections of magazines and newspapers.

- Do an IT skills course: either at your local education authority or privately, but, as above, these aren't cheap.

- Do a business plan, including a summary, market analysis, what the product or service is, about the people, who you are, relevant skills, qualifications and experience, costing and pricing, cash flow forecast, profit and loss account. Your bank manager or accountant will help you with your basic business plan and you can add the additional information.

- Do a marketing plan, giving information about customers, competitors, operations.

- Be aware of any health or legal regulations attached to your business idea. Contact your local trading standards officer, local authority, planning office and chamber of commerce for details.

- Involve your bank manager and your accountant right from the start. Many of them will enjoy your enthusiasm and being part of your dream. Their down-to-earth guidance is often valuable and will give you a taste of what's to come.

- Think about start-up capital. There are four main sources of business funding: your own money (statistics show that a business funded by its owner has the greatest chance of success); loans from relatives, banks or other financial institutions; grants and schemes; venture capital companies.

- Study the competition. The question to answer is 'Will I be able to compete with those businesses already in the market?'

- Sleeping partners are great if you can find them. These are people who put capital into a business and take payment when the business is showing a profit, but they have no interest in the running of the company. All partnerships should be formed legally.

- Don't underestimate your financial requirements. Make sure your business plan includes an accurate cash flow forecast.

- Don't go to a bank to borrow money until you have done your research. They will want to see your business plan, cash flow, marketing research and the product. You should know whether you want a loan or an overdraft, for how long, and when and how you can pay it back.

Types Of Small Business

A small business can include anything from manufacturing and retail to servicing and finance.

PORTFOLIO CAREER

A portfolio career is working for more than one employer. For a lot of areas of employment, such as consultancy, architecture, surgery and teaching, this is the new way of working. For others, such as accountants, cleaners, decorators and people working in the media and communications, it's the way they have always worked. With a portfolio career there is no limit to the number of employers you can have at one time, the only restriction is how many jobs you have the time to do. This way of working particularly suits those who are self-employed, freelance or on short-term contracts.

WARWICK WAS a television director. When the recession hit he lost his corporate television business and was forced to take a job teaching a media television course. After a few years he felt that the teaching job was becoming dull and unchallenging, but he realised that because of the technology and manpower changes it was unlikely he could return to working in television, and that the only way for him to survive was to become more flexible and multi-skilled. 'I realised that twenty years ago an organisation took you on and nurtured you. None of this happens any more. So, when I started to look around for an alternative job to teaching, I realised that I wasn't going to be able to find one job, a regular income and full-time employment. Instead I was going to have to do lots of small jobs, some employed on a part-time basis and others self-employed.'

He allowed his full-time teaching job to tail off, but continued teaching regularly part time. He then contacted the governing body that wrote the exam papers that he was using, suggesting that they needed updating. After meeting with them he accepted a regular part-time job writing their exam papers. The same governing body then invited him to join their examination verification board, which he did, also on a regular part-time basis. He then took a third part-time teaching job. He then got a part-time job working as an educational consultant for the National Council for Vocational Qualifications.

Next he contacted his local radio station and got a job presenting and producing weekend programmes, and reading the half hourly local news bulletins. He also started writing occasional pieces for trade magazines that specialised in his area of expertise. He then contacted the BBC Technical Skills Centre and explained that he was interested in training work. He planned an impromptu visit, hoping to get an interview. He did, and convinced them that big businesses were desperately looking for television training and that with his expertise and their equipment he could do it for them. He started by renting a room, a phone and an office in the BBC building. He did his own marketing and used his own media skills to drum up trade.

Two years down the line Warwick now successfully runs the BBC media class training courses on a part-time basis, offering television and radio training to employees of large corporations. These courses are proving to be so popular that Warwick's part-time involvement is gradually becoming full time. He is also involved in making a film funded by the Millennium Commission, which he shoots on a part-time basis throughout the year.

Warwick earns his living from ten different employment sources, all of which are broadly based on his one area of expertise – media communications. 'I decided that this time I wouldn't put all my eggs in one basket, which is what went wrong with my previous business. This time I would spread myself. I don't have a job any more: I have a number of roles in teaching and television training, based on the same skills, and I love every minute of all of them.'

Pros And Cons

One of the many advantages of being a portfolio worker is that you aren't reliant on a single job, in other words if one of your employers lets you go, you have the safety net of the others to fall back on. Having a number of different jobs can also be very stimulating, which is especially important for people who have a low boredom threshold. You may also earn more than if you are working for a single employer, although finances can fluctuate if one of your employers closes down or fires you. But at least you are in control of replacing them with another, if you want to.

Cons are that you must expect to work longer hours because

of the additional paperwork such as invoicing, and you will miss out on staff benefits such as training and pension schemes. Working for more than one person can also involve a lot of travelling from one employer to the next.

Skills And Resources

As well as doing your job you have to be skilled in:

- accountancy

- keeping correct financial records

- marketing

- regular invoicing.

Plus you have to:

- know the job requirements of each different employer

- be highly flexible

- have good organisational skills, diary keeping and prioritising

- network all the time

- be responsible for yourself and your ability to find employment

- have good people skills

- be discreet – working for several different companies in the same field, confidentiality is extremely important

- be highly motivated.

Types of Portfolio work

Portfolio work can include anything, from teaching to retail trades, or a mix of skills that aren't necessarily related. It is best suited to freelance, self-employment and job sharing.

WORKING FROM HOME

There are no official figures for the number of people who work from home, either self-employed or as employees, but it is estimated by British Telecom (BT) that in the UK there are currently over two million, half a million of these being tele-workers (see below). In 1921 only one in every hundred workers were recorded as working from home. The rise in numbers has been rapid, owing to the progress of IT and the recession of the 1980s which forced many people into self-employment. And, according to the CBI and BT, home-based workers are likely to be four times more productive than on-site employees.

Many organisations particularly those specialising in market research, insurance and finance, now employ staff to work from home on computer terminals. They work between twenty-eight and thirty-six hours a week and are paid at the same rate as other employees. They are supervised by regular visits and work is brought to them by courier. In order to adjust to this way of working many organisations have gone in for 'hot desking', where staff don't own either a desk or a workspace, but on their visits to the office make use of any desk that is free.

Pros And Cons

One of the main benefits of working from home is that you don't have the stress and cost of commuting. The average London-based commuter spends 295 minutes a week travelling to and from work. The yearly cost of car commuting is high, with the average commuter travelling 40 miles a day to and from work, spending around £483 per annum on petrol alone, not taking into account the wear and tear on the car. For disabled people and those who are carers, working from home allows them to remain in the job market.

Despite the many advantages of working from home, however, there is a down side. You can feel isolated, because generally home workers work alone with very little outside stimulation and personal contact. This means that if you have a gregarious character, and love the cut and thrust of office life, the gossip, the camaraderie and the team work, you may find homeworking too lonely.

Skills And Resources

If you are a homeworker then you will benefit from having a working area that is away from the rest of your home and family, preferably with a door you can close at the end of your working day. One homeworker worked from his small bedroom, climbing across his bed to get to his drawing board. The fax positioned on his bedside table used to wake him up at night when it would spring into life with messages from the other side of the world. His problem was getting away from the job. 'When you work from home' he said, 'if you're not careful you end up working every day of the week, it starts to feel like seven Mondays, because you can't escape from the job.' If you are having to use the end of the dining-room table and you have small children, you'll spend a lot of time making sure that they aren't touching anything and you'll spend even more time clearing it all away every night, not to mention the time spent setting it all out again the next day.

You may find that you have to work in the evenings when your children have gone to bed to avoid interruptions. This can be exhausting, and if your work involves using noisy equipment, such as an electric sewing machine, it can annoy your neighbours. Ideally you need to have a workspace that enables you to store dangerous equipment, such as sharp blades or tools, safely.

If lack of space is one of your problems, try utilising a garage, garden shed or loft. Check that it's free from damp, as this can damage materials and papers and can also be unhealthy to work in. Check that you can run electricity or whatever you need, and that the space is light and airy. After all you are going to spend most of your working day in there.

Before you start you should look into:

• The cost of setting up an office at home, equipment and utilising space.

- Whether or not you need planning permission.

- If you are a leaseholder does your lease prevent you from using your home as a work place.

- Will you need additional house insurance. Often working from home can invalidate all your existing policies, if you don't inform your house and contents insurance companies. Several insurance brokers offer specialist packages for homeworkers.

- If you employ someone who works with you at home, you must take out insurance to protect your 'staff' against accident or injury on the job.

- If you employ a helper be aware that you may be eligible for their National Insurance stamp and sick pay.

There are a number of working from home schemes negotiated between employers and trade unions where useful guidelines and advice have been produced for members, but there are many informal working arrangements for employees who work at home. For advice on tax and insurance issues speak to your local Citizens Advice Bureau or Social Security office.

Homeworking Jobs

It is not possible to do assembly line work and work which involves large amounts of machinery from home. Work commonly being done from home includes design, education, accountancy, market research, chiropody and architecture.

TELEWORKING

Teleworking involves either working full or part time from home or from a telecottage and communicating with your office electronically rather than in person. It's possible to telework from virtually anywhere, but telecottages provide a resource of computers, scanners, photocopiers and Internet facilities that are available for you to use. The technology of teleworking is very simple and involves linking a fax machine or computer through a modem, so that data can be sent down your phone line. Teleworkers are fast becoming the 'new age nomads' as armed with a mobile phone, pager, dictaphone, cable connectors and a lap-top, they can work anywhere, any time. Location has become secondary to the electronic office.

Teleworking is set to boom and is already popular in France, Germany, Scandinavia and the US. According to one research centre, 70 per cent of the six hundred UK companies they questioned said they would be implementing it within the next few years.

Some teleworkers, such as Mavis, are supplied with equipment by their employers, 'I have a terminal connected to a modem to a computer company and I ring up and dial in. If I have a technical problem I ring up the technical expert at the main office. I have now met most of the people that I talk to down the line.' Mavis is paid an hourly rate and sends in time sheets to her employer because her hours vary. She has to work at least twenty hours a week. Teleworkers can also be freelance and buy their own equipment. It is usual for freelancers to be commissioned by companies and paid by the job. If the work is continuous then payment is monthly or by the screenful.

Teleworking, like all types of homeworking, doesn't suit everyone's personality. For example, Celia is a teleworker who puts information into the Britsh Telecom Prestel system, 'I find it can get very lonely. The only time I meet other people is through the PTA meetings at school. I have friends who do the same type of work and sometimes I go and see them, but if they are busy working it isn't convenient. Friends come and see me, but if I'm busy I have to sadly turn them away.'

If you are considering teleworking go through the following checklist with your employer.

- You should be supplied with the communications equipment necessary for the job.

- You should be paid for the use of your own heating and lighting.

- You should be paid for when you have to travel to the central office.

- You should agree the hours that you will work and an hourly rate for working them.

- The company you work for should have a proper teleworking policy, so that everyone, managers and teleworkers, understands fully what is expected of them.

- If you are teleworking for a large company you should be given a job specifications list, so that you know exactly what is expected of you. For example, telesales agents could be expected to deal with so many numbers of calls per shift, while word processing and data entry operators could be judged on their daily output.

- Be aware of company security and agree to take responsibility for keeping your 'home office' secure.

Before you start teleworking you should be given some training by your employer with the technology that you will be using. If you are working as a freelance then you will have to train yourself by attending an IT course.

Pros And Cons

The flexibility of teleworking allows you time for your family. If you are a carer this is important. You are available should anything happen to your children or those you care for. You don't have to commute, which can make your working day less stressful and save you money. You don't have to work in unpleasant office conditions. You can also cut costs by not having to buy canteen lunches, snacks and smart working clothes.

You should bear in mind that 28 per cent of teleworkers do not enjoy their working situation as much as those working in offices. Some of the cons of teleworking are:

- no workplace social life, which can be stimulating and continue outside of the office

- loss of colleagues' expertise – you may miss the brainstorming, tossing ideas around, immediate clarification of work problems

- isolation and being trapped at home – like all homeworkers teleworking can be lonely

- reduced training opportunities

- reduced promotion opportunities

- reduced information input

- you need a room to work in without interruption

- difficulty with working routine as you have to be self-motivated and create your working environment and schedule.

See also the information on homeworkers above.

Skills And Resources

When companies are recruiting teleworkers they are looking for:

- interpersonal skills

- listening skills

- verbal reasoning

- an ability to work away from the mainstream of office activity

- ability to follow instructions

- skills in data input

- skills in call handling.

Note also that:

- teleworkers need to be self-motivated, regardless of whether they are working for themselves or as part of a large organisation

- there are tests that can define if you are going to be suitable for teleworking which can be helpful to both you and your employer

- your job should be clearly defined

- keeping in touch with whoever is managing you is essential.

Teleworking Jobs

Teleworking suits the following areas of employment:

- clerical and secretarial

- computer programming

- bookkeeping

- accountancy

- equipment monitoring and maintenance

- graphics

- estimating

- invoicing

- auditing

- telesales.

VOLUNTARY REDUCED WORK TIME

V-time, as it is known, has been operating in the US since 1976. It was introduced in the UK in 1984 and by 1989 1.9 per cent of the workforce were taking advantage of it. There are various employment schemes that allow people to voluntarily trade income for time off. In principle they are given the option of reducing full-time working hours and pay, usually between 5 and 50 per cent, for an agreed specified period, generally between six months or a year, with the right to return to normal working at the end of the agreed period.

Pros And Cons

The benefits of V-time, to both managers and workers, is that it allows you the time off to do whatever you choose. If you are a carer it can solve a lot of problems; it's useful to students because it gives them additional time to study; or you may need time to deal with a family crisis or take a holiday. You can do anything you want with the time off, knowing that your job is there when you return with your employee benefits intact. New technology is changing fast, so before you return to your job you must make sure that your skills are up to date. Once you have agreed the amount of time off that you are taking, you must plan what you are going to do during that time and not allow it to drift away.

Skills And Resources

• You need to be flexible.

• You must organise your time off.

• You must prioritise and pre-plan.

FLEXI-TIME

Flexi-time was first used in West Germany and spread to the UK in the 1970s, and is now very much a normal part of employment practice worldwide. It allows you to be flexible with your working hours within set limits, so you can choose when your day starts and ends. Flexi-leave is possibly the most attractive element of this form of working. It means that you may be able to take credit hours off in core time. There is usually a limit to the number of days or half days that you can take off, or some flexi-leave can be added to your annual holiday. The accounting period for flexi-time is normally one month, with some flexibility to carry credit or debit hours over to the next accounting period. Overtime (any time worked in excess of the standard working day), if agreed, will be authorised, registered and paid for.

Employers have found that flexi-time creates a greater sense of responsibility and commitment from employees, and since people are arriving at different times they tend to get to their work quicker and spend less time on socialising. It's also used to allow companies such as banks, building societies, DIY stores, supermarkets and call centres to extend their opening times.

Pros And Cons

One of the big advantages of flexi-time is that it allows you greater freedom to organise your working hours to suit your personal needs. For example, if both of you are working, one full time and one part time and you have a child in nursery school, flexi-time means that both of you can share the responsibility for your child, by one of you taking him to nursery school in the mornings and the other collecting him in the afternoons.

Working flexi-time also means that you can travel outside peak times to and from work. This means that fares are often cheaper, less traffic means lower fuel consumption, plus you miss the rugby scrum on the train or the bus and can arrive at work feeling less stressed. You can also work in a way that suits your own rhythm, so that if you choose to stay late to finish something, you know that you are accumulating credit you can use later. The added advantage of working at the beginning or end of the the day is that it can be easier to concentrate when there aren't any ringing telephones and there are fewer people around.

Skills And Resources

- You need to be able to take responsibility for your own work.

- You need to be able to pre-plan your working hours.

- You need to be aware of your working rhythms, when you are at your best.

- You need to be flexible.

Flexi-time Jobs

Routine office work and administrative work are highly suitable for flexi-time working. These include jobs in banks, building societies, DIY stores, supermarkets, insurance companies, council administration and the health service.

ANNUAL HOURS

Annual hours, as defined by ACAS (Advisory Conciliation and Arbitration Service), means 'a system whereby employees commit themselves to a number of hours and a pattern of working over a twelve-month period as determined by the needs of the business'. Annual hours can involve employees working longer days in rush periods for no overtime payment which is compensated for by shorter or fewer days when production slows down. The total hours worked is then balanced over a full year.

The system was devised in Scandinavia to create flexibility and first appeared in the UK in the 1950s. In the last twenty years it has become more popular owing to the changing patterns of work, where there is a move away from manufacturing towards service-based industries and there is no longer the need for people to be at a particular place at a particular time. It has also been recognised that giving people some choice about the hours they work improves their motivation and therefore their productivity.

Pros And Cons

The benefits are that you can work more at some times of the year and less at others. You can work when you like to and then take blocks of time off and it can offer the potential of greater income stability and higher guaranteed pay over the year.

The downside is that staffing levels may be reduced, as may overtime payments, and because of the seasonal nature of some employment it can mean that you are expected to work longer hours at certain times of the year, which can be particularly difficult for those who are carers.

Skills And Resources

• You need to be flexible.

• You must be able to work additional hours at short notice.

Annual Hours Jobs

The UK Department of Employment estimated that around 2 million employees, 9 per cent of the workforce in the UK, work on an annual hours basis. The largest proportion, 15.8 per cent, were in professional occupations, with a high number in teaching, followed by plant and machine operators, and craft-related occupations. Some television companies use annual hours to plug the labour gap in studio production, where there can be intense periods of activity, followed by long periods of inactivity. Supermarkets have also found that it suits their employees. The security industry uses an annual hours framework to plan rotas which are adaptable to twenty-four-hour operations. National Health Service trusts, councils and airlines have all introduced annual hours working.

TERM-TIME WORKING

Many working parents have difficulty fitting in their employment with school holidays, because finding good reliable child care is not easy. Term-time working is a way of solving this because it allows working parents to remain working, as either full or part-time employees, but gives them the right to take unpaid leave of absence during the school holidays, which are roughly around thirteen weeks a year, compared to the four or five weeks' annual paid holidays that most employed people are allowed to take.

Pros And Cons

The plus points of term-time working are:

- it's highly suitable for people who have school-aged children, as it relieves the problem of holiday child care

- it suits people who want to do holiday adult education courses

- it gives you the ability to plan your time off

- the time off is longer than other areas of employment.

The down side is:

- loss of income because you don't get paid during the long holidays

- the long unpaid holidays can be boring and unsatisfying.

Skills And Resources

If you are interested in term-time working you must agree with your employer how much unpaid leave from work you require. This will vary depending on how much paid annual leave is available, how long the school holidays are and whether alternative care arrangements can be made for some of the school holiday time. It will be useful to have an ability to plan ahead as it may be better to make these calculations and agreements with your employer at the beginning of the year.

You must be able to budget your finances because your salary or wages can either be normal for the weeks you work, but there will be no payment for time taken off as unpaid leave, or your employer may prefer to calculate how much is owing for the whole year and then average it out each week or month, so you will continue to receive a regular wage but it will be lower than normal.

Term-Time Working Jobs

Most people working in schools, both teaching and also support staff, such as cleaners, cooks and secretaries, only work during term time, but many civil service and government department employees are also being offered term-time working as an option.

CALL CENTRES

We saw in Part 1 how call centres, where orders and enquiries are taken from customers by phone, are booming in many countries around the world. In the US, for example, 3 per cent of the labour force now work in call centres, compared to only 2 per cent in the motor industry. In Europe the number of people employed at hundreds of call centres is estimated to increase from 500,000 to 750,000 by the end of 1999. A leading firm of business experts predicts that the market for call centre software across the world will pass £2 billion by 2003. Call centres were originally a cost-cutting exercise, because the cost of delivering a service down the phone is roughly ten times cheaper than using a sales force and the customer only needs one phone number for the information they require.

Call centre workers each have their own computer, which acts as a filtering system for the phone calls, as well as bringing up on to the screen customers' details and any other relevant information that the operator may require. Some call centres have as few as ten operators, while others have over a hundred, depending on the size of the operation. And call centres don't just handle enquiries and take orders. For example, one telephone share brokerage that works from a call centre in Birmingham claims to account for one in ten share dealings on the London Stock Exchange and has expanded massively with building society conversions.

Many multinational corporations have moved away from high cost areas of employment and have opened telesales centres in Manchester, Belfast, Glasgow and Newcastle. They also take advantage of different time zones by using call centres in the US and the UK, and these take each other's calls outside of their respective office hours. This has now been extended so that if lines are busy calls are automatically passed from one country to the other. Calls from Sweden and Switzerland are also handled in the UK, out of hours. It won't be long before three call centres positioned around the world will mean that calls can be answered twenty four hours a day.

The freephone number on your parking ticket given to you by a traffic warden in London will be answered in Forres, in the Scottish Highlands. If your computer printer doesn't work, dial the helpdesk on a central London number and a person in Amsterdam may talk you through your problem. The world has already shrunk!

Pros And Cons

Basic call centre work, with little or no training and requiring few skills, is fairly low paid. This type of work generally consists of taking down customer details and passing the information on to someone more knowledgeable. It can be repetitive and non-challenging, but it can also be useful employment if you are a student, a carer who needs to work shifts, if you're topping up your earnings or if you are pursuing another less well paid but loved career, or you are between jobs.

However on the upside, many call centres, such as the new telephone banking, insurance and building society services are now employing high performers, with 80 per cent of the work-force being graduates. Each new recruit has to undergo a six-week training programme which includes product and compliance tests. These jobs are well paid and require a high level of skill. The skills – people based, IT and product – generally tend to be transferable.

By moving out of city centres call centres are bringing employment opportunities to areas where jobs were scarce. An example is the Automobile Association which recently closed all its high street outlets and had taken the work instead to call centres.

Note that call centres do not allow people to work from their homes. An experiment a few years ago with home-based directory enquiry operators did not prove to be cost effective. Many experiments in teleworking have come to the same conclusion;

that people doing repetitive jobs work better in an office situation.

Some companies have tried to break away from the idea of centralised call centres and established 'virtual call centres' that enable mostly women working at home to answer calls linked to a central phone centre and a single contact number. However, these schemes have largely been unsuccessful because for most people one of the pluses of doing this type of work is the interaction with others.

Skills And Resources

Some call centre operators deal with calls that are sales focused, while others handle enquiries from dealers as well as customers. Thus they require different skills, depending on the nature of the in-bound and out-bound calls. Most call centre operators need:

- an ability to be polite, trustworthy, knowledgeable, calming and efficient over the telephone

- to be able to deal with difficult customers, such as the elderly, confused, inexperienced, angry

- to speak foreign languages if necessary

- to have necessary knowledge of banking, insurance, engineering, whatever is applicable to the product

- computer skills

- listening skills.

The majority of companies do not want their operators to sound like scripted robots, reading the words off a computer screen. They are looking for individuals who can make their customers feel like individuals. To achieve this the operator will have a conversation outline to guide them, with potentially useful key dialogue and suggestions about how the conversation may go, but the rest is left to the operator to give that individual spontaneity and enthusiasm to every customer conversation. After the twentieth call that can get difficult.

Call Centre Jobs

Many of the services that used to be carried out in your local high street, such as banking and insurance, computer hardware and software suppliers, travel agents and credit card bookings are now carried out through call centres.

Telephone banking, like insurance claims, customer services, sales, after-sales service, warranty queries, mail order, customer support and many other customer-based services which do not require face-to-face contact are now dealt with by call centres.

On The Move

Wherever you can lay cables you can bring jobs, from the south of England to the north, from one side of America to the other and across the vast continent of Australia, thousands of jobs have been created in areas that were previously employment deserts. This is because rents tend to be low, space is available to house large call centres and there is an easily trained labour force on tap with little outside employment competition. Meanwhile specialist call centres continue to be based in capital cities, such as London which takes advantage of the pool of multi-lingual workers that are available there. Many US corporations are also now using the UK as a base for pan-European call centre operations because they often require bi-lingual staff.

SABBATICALS

A sabbatical is when your employers allow you to take a set length of time off work, either paid or unpaid, which does not affect your annual holiday entitlement. Some organisations, such as the Royal College of Nursing, automatically give their professional staff a sabbatical after a certain length of employment. It's a way that some employers choose to reward their staff, without any strings attached; it's also a way that some employers deal with stress and burnout in the workforce. Workers take sabbaticals because it allows them the time, sometimes paid, sometimes unpaid, to pursue whatever interests they have outside of work. Historically sabbaticals have been used for educational purposes, but now people use the time for an assortment of reasons, both educational and social. Some use the opportunity to recharge their batteries, take stock or refocus their lives while knowing that their job will be there for them when they return.

Sabbaticals are common in the US and Australia where 90 per cent of companies permit unpaid leave. Unpaid sabbaticals are becoming more popular in the UK. For example, after five years of employment the Apple corporation in the UK insists that their employees take a nine-month break, on to which they can add some annual leave. This is to ensure that their staff concentrate on their 'personal development' and return to work with renewed enthusiasm.

Pros And Cons

On the positive side sabbaticals can be used for all sorts of things such as gaining a new work experience, undertaking research, doing voluntary work or going on long-distance travel. You can take a break, which can reduce your stress levels, give you the chance to assess your life and your personal growth, take on extra training which is especially important in the rapid growth of technology or just have more quality time with your family. Perhaps the most important gain is, whatever you choose to do with your time, you have the opportunity to take a break knowing that you will return to work refreshed and enthusiastic.

On the down side your skills may not be up to date when you return to work. You should be aware that during your absence the organisation you work for may have changed its management structure, moved buildings or altered your work schedule. It is also possible that becoming involved in another activity can lead to a loss of enthusiasm for your job.

Skills And Resources

If you are planning a sabbatical you need the following skills:

- forward planning for what you intend to do with your sabbatical

- if the sabbatical is unpaid, you need to research and find funding for what you want to do with the time off

- an ability to keep your skills up to date for when you return to work.

HOME STUDY

Distance learning used to mean correspondence courses, which was learning carried out by post. Then along came television and the Open University and now many individuals use distance learning as a way of getting qualifications and degrees, while companies use it to train their staff without having the cost of sending them away and taking time off work.

For many women distance learning is especially important as it eliminates the child care problems that usually arise from being a college student. Distance learning can be done anywhere and whenever you want, even spread out over a long period. It gives you the opportunity to get that necessary additional qualification, degree or training that will bring your skills up to date, without having to go away from home, using the medium of broadcast television, video and e-mail to bring teachers and students together.

Every year 200,000 people in the UK study with the Open University, plus there are another 5,000 students spread out across Europe and many more throughout the US and Australia (see Useful Addresses). Distance learning is hugely popular in both the US and Australia, because it cuts out the need for people to travel long distances, especially important in large countries where towns are a long distance from one another. The Open University courses are open to all adults and there aren't any entry qualifications or proficiency tests. You are completely free to study anywhere, at any time and many Open University students have done exactly that, from being on an oil platform, in hospital, in a submarine and on warships from Novosibirsk to Singapore.

Many companies sponsor students through degree courses

and diplomas, and it's as if employers are now saying that although they aren't any longer able to offer you a job for life, they are prepared to help you to top up your knowledge by gaining further qualifications, which will make you more employable.

Skills And Resources

- If you are a long distance learner it's better not to hurry your course; learning is less exhausting if you do a little every day and spread it over a length of time.

- Make sure that you have a good tutor who is accessible on the end of a phone, fax or via the Internet, to talk you through your assignments.

- Motivation is the key to success, so make sure that you choose a subject that truly interests you and that you want to succeed at, or when the going gets tough, you'll throw in the towel.

Armed with this information about the wide range of opportunities and ways of working, you now have to weigh up the pros and cons of each one and decide which would fit in with your lifestyle, your family commitments and your available skills. Decide if you would have to retrain, your financial requirements, your role as a carer, if you have a partner how would this affect their way of working, your career plan and your ability to be flexible. For further information and leaflets on alternative ways of working, see the Useful Addresses section at the back of this book.

CHAPTER 7

Downshifting — Upshifting

Haven't we all, at some time or another, dreamt of throwing in our jobs and moving out of town to lead an idyllic country life? I certainly have. Sick of the fast food and the slow traffic, the high stress at work followed by the low rewards, surrounded by job insecurity and powerlessness, escape is something that crosses many minds. So far I have decided not to downshift – to exchange a reduced income for a stress-free life – but I can see the appeal. After all, no one has yet found any correlation between increased income and increased happiness and as many of us know expectations quickly rise to meet rising incomes. No one's last words are 'I wish I'd spent more time at work.'

A RENAISSANCE PHILOSOPHY

The word downshifting was first created in 1994 by the Trends Research Institute in New York which announced at the time that it was 'A new Renaissance philosophy'. This meant that the new downshifters were compared to the hippies and the drop-outs of the 1960s, but this was no 'love-in', 1990s style. Downshifting is very different, because it generally involves high achieving, high salaried, ambitious professionals – the movers and the shakers – making a U-turn with their working lives.

Downshifting is for those of you who don't want to work until you drop and then wonder where your life went. It's for people who are tired of feeling tired, trapped, frustrated, powerless and stressed out, and who have decided to go for a lower salary in exchange for a totally different lifestyle or career, with less hassle and more quality time. It may be that downshifting is not the correct term, as this suggests something negative and spiralling down to nowhere. For many people, being released from their debts and jobs, however high-powered, that have lost the dream element and satisfaction, is an uplifting, upshifting experience.

The Henley Centre for Forecasting found that one in eight people in the UK are prepared to cut their spending in order to achieve this and 6 per cent of those workers have already voluntarily taken steps towards reducing their income.

At one time this 'dropping out' as it was called, was seen as a lack of ambition. But the shifts in employment have been so dramatic in the last two decades – with downsizing, job insecurity and the Rambo school of hiring and firing – that people have begun to realise, in spite of putting all their energies and expertise into a company, their loyalty may not be well rewarded. It isn't surprising that many people have decided to opt out of the fast lane and started to believe that they can exchange some part of their income for a better quality of life. Despite this, downshifting (or should it be upshifting?), remains a middle-class solution to what appears to be a classless problem. We are, after all, social beings who need human companionship and interaction, who require friendships and family. We are not faceless, nameless robots, whose only reason for existing is to satisfy the insatiable greed of company shareholders, as they offer us up to be sacrificed to the great god Work.

THAT IS how Gary felt when his media company, which he had founded and nurtured, was taken over and there wasn't a place for him. 'I didn't know the game that investors play. I just thought that if you did a good job and everyone was happy, you carried on.'

Gary had started a company with city investors. He discovered that they weren't interested in the business as such; they just wanted to see the value of their investment grow and when it had risen by ten times the value, instead of investing further, they decided to sell. At that point, Gary went to outside investors and they ended up owning the company.

Gary decided to invest the one year's salary that he was owed and to downshift. He moved to a modest cottage in the country, where he lives on a small amount of money which he earns by making furniture, a subject he studied at art college. 'I don't want to invest time in playing office politics. I enjoy living in the country. I'm basically an artistic person. I earn very little money but it doesn't matter because I don't have any children and I don't have to pay a mortgage. I'm sure if you work in a high-powered job and get the boot, and you don't want to do gardening and walk the dog, it must be hell. But I can't think of anything more wonderful than gazing at a field of sheep. The nicest thing is I get the chance to enjoy my fantasy.'

VOLUNTARY SIMPLICITY

In the US downshifting is well developed and has become known as voluntary simplicity or planned crossover. A Harvard academic recently conducted a survey at a large US telecommunications firm where 73 per cent of those questioned thought they could spend less and live more simply. Statistically it is true, that despite working longer hours and suffering higher stress, only 5 per cent of workers in the UK are paid enough for a modestly comfortable lifestyle – not enough for a new car, a mortgage over £30,000 or a proper pension – but enough for a comfortable life.

The time and energy it takes to earn this modest income has increased to such an extent that we hardly have time to spend it. This has had a devastating effect on the businesses of the self-employed, who rely on the better off to be their clients and customers. On top of this the cost of housing in the UK has nearly doubled as a percentage of income in the last ten years – from 9 per cent to 16 per cent – the result being that once the monthly mortgage payment has been paid, the remainder of the home budget is very tight.

PRACTICAL TIPS FOR POTENTIAL DOWN-SHIFTERS

If you are thinking of downshifting and moving out of town you should go through the following list before making your decision.

- Visit the area you are thinking of moving to, at high and low season, if possible – ideal picture postcard countryside can be bleak in winter.

- Consider seriously how cut off you want to be – you may find an idyllic remote location makes you feel very isolated.

- Don't make these decisions just after a holiday in the area as you will be looking at it through rose-tinted glasses.

- Look at property prices to see what you can afford.

- Look at the local employment that's available even if it's part-time or odd jobs to keep you active, bring in a small income and enable you to meet new people – blissful silence can become mind numbing.

- The local newspaper will be a mine of information on facilities such as shops, schools, hospitals and recreation facilities.

- Do you need outside social stimulation? Look at the local entertainment facilities. Boredom shouldn't replace stress.

- Discuss practical financial aspects of your downshifting with your accountant or bank manager.

- If you have redundancy money consult an expert about the best ways of investing it so it will give you a small regular income.

- Try to predict your financial future, especially if you are living off a limited income.

- Make a downshifting plan.

- What's the lowest amount you can realistically live on?

- What are you are trying to achieve?

- What support systems do you need? Make a list; you could include family, friends and pets if they are important to you.

- What will you miss?

- What luxuries and comforts can you do without?

- Realise that you now have the chance to enlarge your hobbies.

- If you have medical needs, check that these can be met in an out-of-the-way place.

- Check out whether it's actually just your job that you want to change or whether it's your complete lifestyle.

RACHAEL MADE the decision to leave her £50,000 a year market-ing job, after realising that she had become a 'tired all the time' workaholic, 'From the initial realisation it took a year for me to pluck up the courage to leave my job. I was cushioned by five months savings so the first morning after I'd left I felt totally free.' There followed two years of soul searching and an assortment of part-time jobs, including cleaning, before Rachael finally realised that what she had always wanted to be was a clown. After doing a circus skills workshop where she learnt juggling and riding a unicycle, she sold her flat and is now spending six months training with a bona fide circus.

For many of us it can take either a health or family crisis to force us to change our jobs or the way that we work. Changing jobs can be a difficult decision, which is why redundancy is often described by people as being a 'blessing in disguise', because the decision to leave their job is taken out of their hands.

It is far better if you can to make your own decisions about your own life and not be forced into situations. This is why you should try to stay one jump ahead of your employment situation and do a rain check on the way that you feel about your job, a stress test. Ask yourself if your job is fun, fulfilling, challenging, fascinating, energising and interesting or if it's become stressful, exhausting, dull, repetitious, anxious making, overloaded and unrewarding. If it has, then it's time to seriously start considering your employment options, or looking at alternative ways of working. Don't let the stress get the better of you.

EMPLOYMENT CAREER BREAKS

This form of working was first started by the high street banks and was a perk of the job offered to high-flying women to provide them with a short break, followed by a speedy return to full-time employment, so that the company didn't lose them. Now it has been extended to women who would otherwise leave their jobs to start a family and look after small children. It is also now offered to men.

Employment career breaks are an extended period of unpaid leave. The idea is that at some time in the future the employee will return to work with the same employer, doing the same job, retaining most of their service-related benefits. It also takes on board maternity, paternity, parental and sabbatical leave.

A few years ago the UK's National Health Service introduced career breaks of up to five years for staff to care for children or elderly relatives. A survey carried out by Personnel Today, of 927 organisations found that 12 per cent offered career breaks. Banks and finance firms came out top. A New Ways to Work survey found that 15 per cent of top managers were currently taking a break and 7 per cent had just returned.

Pros And Cons

One of the benefits of taking an employment career break is that it gives you the opportunity to plan a break from work without having to worry that it will interrupt your career and that you will have to find a new job when you return. You also have the opportunity to take extended maternity leave to care for your children until they reach nursery-school age, or you can return to full-time education to get a degree or any other qualification that will improve your future employment status.

The downside is that taking a break like this can affect your pension entitlement. If it involves terminating your contract then this can affect your continuity of employment which may reflect on your conditions of employment. When you return you should be offered a job at the same level as the one you had previously, but there are no such guarantees.

In a world where technology is changing fast a long break could result in you losing touch with highly specialised IT work, so bringing your skills up to date when you return can take longer. To combat this, use some of your time to take a course to upgrade your technological skills, to stop you from falling behind. Some employers also keep their staff on leave up to date with days back to work and training.

PART 3

Survival Skills

CHAPTER 8

Check Your Survival Rating

Complete this quick quiz and get some idea if you have the right
outlook to ride the waves of the changes in employment. Answer
'yes' if you are receptive to the ideas below, 'no' if they do not
appeal to you.

Question Yes No

1. Is a job for life unimportant to you? ☐ ☐

2. Do you think it's impossible to find employment for your lifetime? ☐ ☐

3. Is having a large number of support staff
unimportant to you? ☐ ☐

4. Have you ever done your own secretarial
work? ☐ ☐

5. Do you have basic keyboard skills? ☐ ☐

6. Do you think you'll never be able to retire? ☐ ☐

7. Could you work without your own office? ☐ ☐

8. Is it unimportant where you carry out your
work? ☐ ☐

	Yes	No
9. Do you think you are responsible for your own employment?	☐	☐
10. Do you think your CV should be short and to the point?	☐	☐
11. Do you think networking on the Internet can help your career?	☐	☐
12. Are you prepared to change your job several times during your career ?	☐	☐
13. Do you feel confident about change?	☐	☐
14. Do you think that all jobs require some computer literacy?	☐	☐
15. Do you believe a self-assessment skills audit can help you to change your career?	☐	☐
16. Do you know how to fill a skills gap?	☐	☐
17. Do you consider learning at your workplace is 'real' learning?	☐	☐
18. Do you think commitment to your job is more important than loyalty?	☐	☐
19. Do you turn off your mobile phone when you're busy?	☐	☐
20. Do you let your answer machine answer your phone?	☐	☐
21. Do you answer faxes when it's convenient to you?	☐	☐

Yes **No**

22. If you were being bullied at work would you:
    (a) Allow the bully to provoke you into responding aggressively and deal with it yourself? ☐ ☐
    (b) Take the matter up with your union representative or personnel department? ☐ ☐

23. Do you think putting your CV on the Internet could help to get you a job? ☐ ☐

24. If you haven't any up-to-date skills do you think:
    (a) It's harder to find employment? ☐ ☐
    (b) It won't make any difference because technology is changing so fast? ☐ ☐

25. Would you work part time? ☐ ☐

26. Have you ever re-trained? ☐ ☐

27. Are your skills transferable? ☐ ☐

28. Would you feel comfortable working for a female employer? ☐ ☐

29. Do you know how to use the Internet? ☐ ☐

30. Do you know the difference between the Internet and the Intranet? ☐ ☐

31. Would you enjoy telecommuting? ☐ ☐

32. Do you think you should take any training courses that your employer offers you? ☐ ☐

RESULTS

If you answered **Yes** to:

More than 16 questions   Whether you are employed or job hunting, you are well on the way to understanding how to handle employment and looking for employment in the future. For you re-training, flexible working and the importance of your skills and understanding of the new technology, is not a problem. Keep your stress levels under control. You can trust that answer machine to pick up your calls, and replying to every fax or e-mail instantly isn't necessary.

Between 10–16 questions   You are feeling a little insecure, but you are aware of the changes and are willing to adapt to them. Change isn't easy and the changes in employment have been so dramatic that we are all having to adjust to them. The new technology can also be mind blowing, especially if it has totally changed the working face of your particular job, but it isn't going to go away, in fact in the future it's going to become even more powerful. Don't look upon it as an enemy; it's a working aid, just like the typewriter was to my father and the computer is to me. Going on some IT courses is a huge help and can give you back that feeling of control over your working environment.

It also shows an employer that you are moving forward. If you are looking for employment, don't hang on to that old CV, it probably looks dated and however much it may have stood you in good stead in the past, it's time to dust it down and make it more modern (see Chapter 9). Just changing the layout and reducing it, if possible, to a single page, will give an employer the overall impression that you are a forward thinking person.

Less than 10 questions   You are unaware of the changes in employment or you are sticking your head in the sand, but either way you are going to have to face up to them sooner or later. Make it sooner or you'll be left behind. If you're feeling emotionally battered because you gave your loyalty to your employer and now you've been laid off, well you aren't alone, it's happened to thousands of others. Skills, expertise and commitment are what count now and you have all of those, you just have to look at a new way of using them. Do your own DIY skills audit and it will help you to see just how multi-skilled you actually are. Get advice on your CV, it may need updating (see Chapter 9).

You can't stop change. You can't reverse everything. Employment isn't going to go back to the way that it was. Whatever your age, you are going to have to look at how you now fit into this employment landscape. Your local Job Centre, Job club or employment agency will discuss with you your skills and how they can be adapted. Check out your local adult education centre for IT courses. Look at more flexible ways of working and becoming multi-skilled.

SKILLS AUDIT

Skills assessments are something that colleges and universities do for students fairly frequently. Despite all the obvious benefits, once you have left education and are out in the workforce you very rarely stand back and do a skills audit on yourself, that is until you lose your job or your company goes to the wall, and you are confronted with unemployment and trying to find a way back into the job jungle. Therefore, from time to time, it is a good idea to carry out your own skills audit.

An appraisal of your skills can help you to identify strengths and weaknesses, bridge any gaps and understand how you can diversify. This is important for your employment chances and choices. It turns you into a realistic, multi-faceted, employable worker. Armed with the knowledge learnt from your skills audit, you should be able to fill in the pieces of your own employment jigsaw.

Key Points For Your Successful DIY Skills Audit

Break down your skills into three categories:

• Practical   (for example, rebuilding cars, cooking, gardening)

- Intellectual   (for example, IT knowledge, financial, legal)

- Personal   (for example, people skills, listening skills).

Don't undervalue yourself:

- Spend time on your skills audit, you won't remember all your skills at once.

- Don't disregard what you consider are everyday skills, such as driving, being a good listener, house decorating, basic IT skills, good team player.

- Get reliable feedback, ask friends, relatives and work colleagues what alternative careers they think you could do, but to do this successfully you need unbiased opinions.

- Think about what careers might interest you, however off the wall or out of character.

- Match your skills to jobs you see advertised.

- Make a note of any skills gaps you may have. Consider how you can fill them.

- Apply for a wide range of jobs and don't restrict yourself to one area of employment.

- Send off for job application forms.

- Always contact the employers and ask for the job specifications before applying for a job.

- Your local careers office can help you do your skills audit. They can also be a very useful sounding board if your ego is feeling beaten down from a recent job loss and you're finding it hard to value your skills as highly as you should.

- Read trade papers and magazines and go to trade shows which cover your area of expertise. Keep up to date with what is happening in that particular area.

- Go to trade shows and read trade magazines and newspapers in areas of employment that you want to move into, or that interest you. You'll find that your local library will carry the majority of trade journals.

- Multi-skilled means flexible – it makes you capable of doing a mixed bag of jobs and broadens your employment platform.

- Look for gaps in the employment market. You may find a weak area where you could offer some expertise.

HOW TO BE MULTI-SKILLED

- Do a skills audit on yourself.

- Several small, part-time jobs, each paying you a small amount of money can be stimulating and add up to you being well paid overall.

- Explore whether it's possible to channel your interests or hobbies into employment. For example; if your hobby is gardening you could become a garden designer. If you enjoy cooking you could go into catering.

- Take a piece of paper and draw a large circle on it. Write your core skill in the centre of the circle and then fill the remaining space with other employment areas which branch off from your main area of expertise. In my case writing for magazines branched into writing for newspapers, then books and finally writing for television. Teaching can become private tutoring, adult evening classes, writing education books. Banking skills can be transferred into accountancy or the role of a financial advisor.

- If you have a multi-skilled base (ie if you have more than one core skill), draw two intersecting circles and see if any of your skills overlap – generally you'll find that they do.

CHAPTER 9

Preparing Yourself for Change

You've done the background work, so now you are at the point where it's time to start writing your CV, networking, making job applications and going for interviews. Your mind should now focus on how to sell yourself. Regard yourself as a product and ask yourself why should someone buy you or, in other words, hire you? By now you should be able to answer that question positively and successfully. Armed with that information about yourself, you are ready to move forward.

YOUR CV

Whatever the job, from film runner to executive, working full time, part-time or job sharing, an employer expects you to have a CV or a resumé. It's your calling card. It allows you to put your working life and achievements on paper.

If you think composing a CV is easy then why does everyone, at one time or another, get it wrong? The answer is because it's hard to make it lean, mean, pacey, punchy and full of hire-me credentials. It takes preparation and an ability to tailor it to each prospective employer. It's the one opportunity you have to really blow your own trumpet. The employment guru Charles Handy believes that CVs have a lousy track record, that most of them end up in the bin and that they are self-defeating, in the sense that they make job seekers feel they're doing something, when in fact all they're doing is getting rejected from a distance. Well, at least that is nicer than being rejected face to face.

Of course he has a point, but on the other hand we live in a working world where most employers, job advertisements, agencies and head hunters want to see your CV before they see you. It's not what you do, it's the way that you do it. If you send out your CV cold, with no research, no preparation, just aiming it at the wall, thinking that any old company in the phone book or the trade directory will do, but at least it shows that you're job hunting, then the bin is probably where your CV will end up. You'll be screened out before you even get started, for all sorts of reasons:

- you sent it to a company at random, where they aren't hiring, in fact they may well be downsizing

- you sent it to a company that doesn't require your type of skills, expertise or experience

- you didn't tailor your CV to suit the market you are aiming at

- your CV was a mess – wrong spelling/badly laid out

- you told employment lies and sooner or later you'll get found out. There is little point in saying that you have a skill when you don't, thinking that when it comes to it you'll be able to wing it, because you won't. Skills have to be performed and if you can't do them then you won't get the job or, if you do, you certainly won't keep it

- you sent your CV to the wrong person within the company and they have either left, been promoted or aren't in the position of hiring.

- you didn't get a job specification before applying for the job

- your CV was too long and out of date.

Don't send a CV that's going to end up in the rubbish bin. In order for your CV to work for you have to:

- target it – your skills should fit the company and the job

- research the company, the management and the product, so you are sure of the skills they are looking for

- make your CV lean, mean and pacey, no longer than two sides of A4 paper

- write it directly for the job in question

- always send a specifically tailored covering letter saying something that you know about the organisation and what it does, and perhaps praise something the company has done recently

- also include information about the benefits to your previous company of the work you did.

Also, remember:

- don't try and be humorous

- make it easy-to-read, plain and simple no fancy borders and typefaces

- never mention your primary school

- don't use phrases like: 'Good at organisation and arranging meetings', it's too general – you need to give examples that demonstrate those qualitites

- don't use etc, etc – it's too vague, be more specific.

The key points in a CV that you want to get across to an employer are: your best qualities, highlights of your background, your training and skills, your job experience and your qualifications.

Have a copy of your CV ready at your interview to remind you of certain points that your interviewer may want to discuss. Once on paper and set in order, you will find it easier to talk through the key points of your career and your skills. You may find it helpful to highlight sections you think are particularly relevant to the job. Having your CV with you gives you the dates and facts at your finger tips, so you don't have to make fumbling guesstimates.

Remember the main point of a CV is to do the most brilliant selling job for you. One of the three different types listed below, together with their pros and cons, will be the most effective showcase for your skills. Whichever you choose the most important point is that your CV should be clear and concise.

The Three Types Of CV

Chronological
A chronological CV lists your work experience in reverse order starting with your current job. This is the most commonly used type of CV. It works well if you have a long, strong work history and if you are remaining in the same area of employment and career structure. However, one of the drawbacks of this type of CV is that it doesn't give you the opportunity to highlight some of your skills, which may be more interesting to the employer than others, plus it shows up any gaps in your work history.

Functional
A functional CV highlights your best skills and plays down any lack of work experience. This type of CV is particularly useful for students, ex-offenders, returners or those with little work experience. If you have strong work experience this type of CV does not allow it to shine through.

Chronological and Functional
A combination CV allows you to be versatile with your information and does a good selling job on your talents. This type of CV is useful if you have had a mixed career with an assortment of jobs. But remember that with this type of CV you must lay it out thoughtfully, choose your words carefully and don't get too flowery.

What To Include

Regardless of the type of CV you send, remember you are the product that you are selling, and that you are competing with other CVs, job application letters, business and junk mail. Make your layout and typeface clear and easy to read. Don't go for tinted or patterned paper, use good-quality white paper and envelopes. To grab the reader's attention the top half of the opening page of your CV should have the following:

- A clear summary of your qualifications. If there are particular qualifications required for the job, then put those first.

- List your strongest skills.

- If your education is important to the job, list it now, if not then leave it until later.

- Make sure the companies that you have worked for in the past can be easily picked out and briefly explain the service they offered.

- Make sure the positions that you held in those companies are also clear.

- Don't gloss over any employment gaps. If there has been a gap then you should say. Don't give the reasons – you can do that if the question arises at the interview.

- Being made redundant isn't unusual now and isn't any longer an employment slur. The person who is interviewing you may well have once been in the same situation.

Style points
- Keep paragraphs short.

- Don't use a typeface that's too small.

- Always type your CV – don't hand write it.

- Keep the overall length to one page, at a maximum two.

- Check your spelling.

- Use bullet points and sub headings to break up the text.

- Overall layout should be neat and easy to read.

- Don't use eradicator pens.

Tailoring Your CV

To have the maximum effect your CV should be tailored to the company you are contacting and the job you want. There is little point in just writing everything down in the same order for everyone as the details won't be relevant to every single job. You have to bring the right skills and abilities to the attention of the right employer. You have to make the employer need you. To do this you must research the organisation as thoroughly as you can.

- Look up the organisation in various trade directories, available at your local library.

- Look at the size of the company, its turnover, number of employees, the area it covers, if foreign languages or other skills are important to the business.

- Buy the organisation's product.

- Call the company, and ask for any brochures, job specifications or written information available.

- Keep up to date by reading any articles about the company in trade and business magazines or newspapers.

- Look up the company's Web page, to find out how the company sees itself and what its values are.

- If the company is involved in the media, watch its TV programmes/films/listen to its radio shows/read its books/ magazines/newspapers/advertisements.

Always accompany your CV with a hand-written covering letter and mention something about the product that the company produces (or the service they provide), either in a way that shows how it matches your skills, experience or interests, or mention something about it that you admire, want to work with or be involved in, but don't get over flowery. Whatever aspect of the business you comment on, make sure you can back this up at an interview, to show you've really done your background research and checked out the competition.

What You Should Not Put On Your CV

There are certain things that you should *not* include on your CV. Here's a checklist of important **do nots.** Do not:

- send a photograph of yourself

- give your salary past or present

- list your references

- give your age

- list your children or their ages

- give your marital status

- give your weight, height, sex, race

- list your hobbies, unless they are in some way related to the job or to your skills

- give your reason for leaving your present employment

- say whether you are in employment at the present time

- write about yourself in the third person.

When You Don't Get A Reply

At one time or another we have all sent off a CV, sometimes cold, but often in reply to a job advertisement and never received a reply. Getting a rejection is something you're probably prepared for, but being left 'up in the air' not knowing can be difficult to deal with.

The UK Institute of Personnel and Development has had a recruitment code called 'The IPD Guide on Recruitment' since 1978. It states that 'unsuccessful candidates must always be notified in writing as soon as a decision is reached'. It goes on to say that 'receipt of solicited applications must always be acknowledged. Unsolicited applicants should also be acknowledged whenever possible.' This may be the code, but many organisations don't practise it.

Always keep a list of who you have sent your CV to, the date it was sent and which type of CV. After about a week to ten days if you don't get a response to your CV, ring the organisation you sent it to. Be polite; after all they may still give you a job. Speak to the person who you sent your CV to or their assistant, say that you are checking to see if they received it as you haven't had a reply. If they haven't received it, offer to send another. If they have, ask if there is any chance of a meeting.

JOB ADVERTISEMENTS

If you are answering a job vacancy advertisement, you should also research the organisation and comment about their product in your covering letter. You can do this by looking them up in various trade directories available in your local library, through the newspaper or if the product is available going out and finding it. Always look at the competition. If possible match your skills and qualifications to those listed in the job description and to that specific area of employment. Adapt your CV to fit. If there is one available, always get the job specification.

Job advertisements, both in the press and at employment agencies, frequently use abbreviations for job descriptions as well for the job itself. Here are some of the more widely used abbreviations you'll find in job advertisements with their definitions:

AAE	according to age and experience
c. or *circa*	around/approximately
CAM	computer aided manufacturing
CNC	computer numerical control
EPOS	electronic point of sale
FX	foreign exchange
IT	information technology
IWS	integrated work stations
LAN	local area network
Neg	negotiable
OTE	on target earnings
PA	per annum

PA	personal assistant
SMT	surface mounted technology
TQC	total quality control

THE INTERVIEW

Generally getting a job involves getting through one or more interviews. Sometimes you will have to first undergo an in-depth interview, usually on a one-to-one basis, followed by interviews for those who have been short-listed. These can either be one or more one-to-one meetings with different people, or a panel interview. Both will usually involve more senior members of the management.

If you are offered an interview always check beforehand whether the company is paying your travelling expenses. The IPD guide says that organisations should be prepared to pay reasonable expenses for candidates to attend interviews. This is especially important to students and returners who often go for many interviews when they first leave college, which can involve travelling many miles.

If the interview will include psychological testing (see below), you will have been told beforehand. If you haven't been told you are to be tested in advance, then you can refuse to do it, and offer to return to sit it at another time, when you are more prepared.

Some employers will give you the opportunity to see the type of job you are applying for actually being done at the company and to meet those involved. If you are offered this opportunity, always accept it and when you are taken round, look, learn and listen – you can only gain further insight into the job and the organisation and this will give you additional ammunition when it comes to asking questions at the end of the interview.

When you go for an interview the first and often the most important impression you can give about yourself comes across in the first few minutes by the way that you dress and your general image, self-confidence and opening words.

The last minute of the interview generally determines the

outcome, so don't let your guard down. Ask a range of questions and check when you expect to hear about the results of the interview. Don't be fobbed off with, 'We'll let you know'.

Interview Dos and Don'ts

Dos:

- Plan your journey. Do a dummy run the day before if you aren't sure of the way.

- Look smart; it'll help you to feel good and feeling good gives added confidence.

- Be sure you have done your research on the organisation, the job and the market area.

- Have a copy of your CV with you to give you the key dates and facts of your career at your fingertips, highlight certain areas you feel are important to bring up.

- Shake hands in a firm and friendly way.

- Smile.

- Listen.

- Speak clearly, enthusiastically and with huge amounts of confidence.

- When answering questions be precise and keep to the point.

- Remember your body language, sit in a friendly, open, yet businesslike way.

- Sit still.

- Give yourself plenty of time, so that you don't have to cut the interview off early.

- Always send a letter of thanks afterwards.

Don'ts:

- Don't be late.

- Don't arrive cluttered down with bags, unless you have been asked to bring examples of your work.

- Don't give a limp handshake.

- Don't let any nervous ticks that you may have get out of control.

- Don't smoke.

- Don't swear.

- Don't criticise your former employer.

- Don't mumble.

- Don't fidget.

- Don't be too serious.

- Don't chew gum.

High-Tech Interviewing

At an interview, you should be prepared for more than just a cosy chat. Remember your body language. These days you could be putting your whole psyche on the line. Two-thirds of organisations admit that their recruitment processes are more structured than they were and an increasing number of companies are using various techniques to sift through applicants and process the skills and reliability of interviewees. These techniques range from panel interviews and requests to see samples of work, to the use of computers to read job applications which pick out key words.

Solid city companies such as Barclays Bank and the Halifax Building Society in the UK currently use psychological testing as part of their recruitment procedures and are convinced that, together with interviews, they are a good source of secondary information with the ability to predict a person's future work performance. Psychological testing is very popular with employers in The Netherlands, the US and Australia. One of the largest companies specialising in psychological testing boasts sixty-two clients out of the US Fortune Top 100, as well as seventy out of the UK FTSE 100 and half of the biggest companies in The Netherlands. Indeed, 75 per cent of organisations with more than 1,000 employees now use psychological tests when it comes to recruiting new staff.

Psychological Testing

Psychological testing or profiling measures intelligence and aptitude. There are a wide variety of tests, ranging from complex scientific personality inventories, to basic work sampling for keyboard skills. As a guideline the UK Institute of Personnel and Development defines psychological tests as 'tests which can be systematically scored and administered, which are used to measure individual differences for example in personality, aptitude, ability, attainment or intelligence, are supported by a body of evidence and statistical data which demonstrates their validity and are used in an occupational setting'.

The tests evaluate your psychological profile under such categories as 'Relationships with people', 'Thinking style', 'Feelings' and 'Emotions'. A test sample asks you to give the most appropriate response to statements such as 'I am the sort of person who . . .', 'Choose from the following four responses: Assertive in groups; Applies common sense; Can sell ideas; Manages to relax easily'.

For the job hunter this can be powerful stuff. After all, you could find the difference between getting a job or not is whether you agree or disagree with such questions as 'I enjoy meeting people', 'I'm easily disappointed' or 'I sometimes make mistakes'. This type of testing is virtually standard practice in graduate recruitment, but it is beginning to be used across the board, not just in selecting managers, but also in choosing secretaries and administrative personnel.

Our personality traits apparently put us into various set categories, which bear little similarity to one another. For example, air-traffic controllers do not show the same characteristics as foreign-exchange dealers, and there are few similarities between captains of industry.

If a future employer or your present employer who is considering putting you forward for training, asks you to sit one of these tests, you should:

• be given advance notice of the test

• be fully informed of the reasons why you are sitting the test

• be told what type of test you are sitting

• be told the length of the test.

You may be given some practice papers beforehand so that you can familiarise yourself with the tests. You should check that the test results are scored, interpreted, evaluated and communicated by trained personnel, who if they don't have the British Psychological Society Statement or Certificate of Competence should be supervised by someone who does. You should be told how the information you give will be used and stored and given the opportunity to receive feedback on the results.

Can You Cheat?

Of course it's possible to cheat by giving false answers to the questions, but it would only work if you knew the kind of personality profile the job requires. The scoring of these tests can be very complex and depends on what the test is attempting to measure. Some tests are looking at general ability, such as number skills and tests of attainments such as spelling. Other tests are solely comparative and have no right or wrong answers. These present a profile of each individual and include personality and interests. Other forms of tests may be designed in-house and include structured group discussions, individual creative work, job analysis questionnaires and work sampling. The person assessing you during these actitivies – or the results – judges whether you have been successful or not.

The Virtual Interview

There are occasions when the interviewer and the person that they are interviewing are unable to get together. The way of eliminating distance is to hold an interview 'down the line' using the Internet. This involves two computers both equipped with a small camera and microphone. Unfortunately both the pictures and the sound are being squeezed through telephone lines so the result tends to be jerky pictures and fuzzy sound. Most interviewers in this situation make allowances for the circumstances. You can also take psychological tests on the Internet.

It's going to be about another ten years before this system of interviewing will have been perfected. Meanwhile, for the near future the majority of interviews will continue to be held face-to-face.

If, however, you are involved in a virtual interview try to behave as naturally as possible as if the person interviewing you is sitting opposite you. Treat the camera as if it were the interviewer. It could be helpful to practise your virtual interview technique with a friend interviewing you using a video camera.

NETWORKING

When you're looking for a new job or a career change there's a tendency to be so centred on the new technology – Do I know how to work it? Should I update my skills? Will I be able to get a job because of it? – that there's a danger of underestimating the strengths and job-finding potential of good old-fashioned networking. It's still one of the most important basic tools of job hunting, especially in a world where paternalism is all but dead and short-term contracts, flexibility and self-reliance are all fast becoming keys to employment. Some people just dismiss networking as an 'old boys network', thinking that it only works for ageing bank managers, dozing in leather armchairs in some dusty gentlemen's club, and that the CV and the Internet will be sufficient to get you a job. They might, but so will networking. Combine all three job-finding tools and you seriously increase your job-finding chances. Job hunting is like a main meal, you need additional side dishes to make it a success.

What is so brilliant about networking is that it's part of you; it's part of all of us. Your own network is something you can build, and if you nurture it it will grow and help you to either make a career change, find a job or insure against future redundancy. It doesn't matter if you are working part time, a middle manager or executive, male or female, young or middle aged, networking works. Research proves it: 70 per cent of all jobs that were filled in the UK in 1997 were never advertised.

Networking isn't just about what you know. Everyone you have ever met has the potential to be a contact in your networking.

Your Networking Plan

Spread the news that you are available for work. Target organisations and people who would be interested in someone with your talents and expertise. Don't overlook:

- People you play sports with.

- Your neighbours.

- Parents of your children's school friends whom you meet daily in the playground.

- Parent Teacher Associations, local committees, societies.

- Friends and past work colleagues. Don't overlook or hesitate to make the most of the goodwill that you have built up at your last place of employment.

- Trade unions and associations involved with your area of work.

- Bank manager, vicar, priest, relatives, doctor, accountant, evening class colleagues, even your milkman. I know someone who got their job from a contact known to their shared milkman, so don't rule anyone out.

Research shows that most people can list between one and two hundred people as contacts, working on the 'everyone you've ever met' criteria, not just those on your Christmas card list.

Another way of widening your network is to join one of the Common Purpose programmes that have been set up around the country. They are based on US community schemes for people aged between thirty and forty-five, who work in the private, public and voluntary sectors. The programme consists of a two-day residential workshop, plus nine days of intensive seminars covering issues such as crime, education, health and housing. A management consultant who recently finished one of the programmes says it was an eye opener, 'I met people I would otherwise never have had a chance to meet. I discovered how the City works, where the levers are to get things done. I have also had professional opportunities that I wouldn't ever have had and I can now enjoy a wider network of contacts, not just in my own area but throughout London.' Another participant estimated that it would have taken him ten years to find the people he now knows through going on one of these courses.

Casting Your Net

- Network across your industry and you will find out not only what is going on, but also what the job and promotional opportunities are.

- Through networking you can also be warned about companies that are heading for problems. This type of information could be an advantage or disadvantage, but remember either way that all knowledge is power, especially when you are trying to make a decision about your future employment.

- Contacts found through networking are able to introduce you to people who work in specific companies and they can introduce you to specific work opportunities. Networking means that you are in a position for people to pass you on to their own contacts, which gives you another layer to network.

Networking Tips

Here are the keys to good networking:

- Don't just target everyone you have ever met indiscriminately. Only target those people who you know admire you, and who like and understand what you do. They don't necessarily need to have a complete understanding of all your skills and your business, but they do need to like you. For example, if your previous employer was forced to let you go when they didn't want to and you know that they admired your talents, while they are still feeling guilty and sad about you leaving, it might be a very good idea to ask their advice on whom you might contact.

- If you've just lost your job, it's also a good time to ask your colleagues and co-workers for their advice.

- If you are in a downsizing or mass redundancy situation then firing in numbers can result in shared anxiety and anger on the one hand, but on the re-employment front a feeling that it's everyone for themselves can prevail so people become very secretive and not willing to share any contacts because they don't believe that there are enough jobs to go round.

- After massive lay offs there's the initial shock and resentment among workers, with the overwhelming thought, 'They don't care about us, why should we care about them?' syndrome. But sooner or later someone comes into the office with the news that they have a job. Instantly people perk up and start to believe that they can do it too and the unemployment lethargy seeps away to be replaced by the competitive survival instinct. In this scenario some amount of networking between your own colleagues can be helpful. You mustn't imply that you are picking their brains so you can steal their leads, in fact you should stress the opposite. But swapped information about who has tried where and what the response was, helpful literature, organisations and directories can be very useful and constructive.

- There is a camaraderie about networking among people who are all in the same employment situation. For example, when ex-offenders are released from prison they are known to find employment through their own network of ex-offenders quicker than those using the normal employment channels.

Developing Relationships

The foundations of good networking are the relationships that you develop. This involves:

- concentrating on becoming more valuable to others

- not just assessing how valuable people are to you, as a good networker assesses how valuable others are and how they can fit into both your and other people's networks, making you a broker for lots of people, so you become part of people's lives

- telling potential employers about your network – if you are well connected it could be one of the reasons for hiring you.

Women Networking

Many people in the communications business believe that women are better at networking than men. If there is any substance in this idea, it's probably because women tend to be very good at collaborating and working in teams, and more in tune with their intuitive side.

One of the biggest problems women have in networking is that they simply don't get invited to places where they are able to network. After all, if you aren't there, you can't network.

Overcoming Networking Fear

If you're one of those people who find it not just tricky but really painful to walk into a room full of strangers, even in a social setting, then networking is going to take a little bit more effort from you. If the very idea of having to sell yourself, however softly, makes you cringe then stand back and look at the situation.

An alternative to networking, which doesn't involve any face-to-face meetings, is to send up a plane and put it up there in sky writing – who you are and what kind of employment you're looking for. This method would reach thousands of people, without a doubt, maybe some of them might even be potential employers, but would your message in the sky have that human touch? Would they be able to see you? Could they hear you holding their interest as you explained to them, with all that passion and skill, what you do and why you want to do it? It would deprive a future employer of any personal judgement of you which might be relevant to the job, such as the following questions.

- Do you have the potential to do the work?

- Do you have the personality to be part of a team?

- Are you better working alone out on the road?

- Are you a good listener?

- Are you a charismatic talker?

- Do you have the ability to think fast and make vital decisions on the spot?

- Are you reliable and keen?

- Can you motivate a workforce?

- Do you take responsibility?

- Can you make judgements?

- Are you open to new techniques?

- Are you flexible and can handle change?

These are just some of the things we learn about people when we talk to them face-to-face. The sky writing, for all its razzmatazz, fails to deliver on all of those counts, whereas networking is people based and people are the bedrock of any organisation.

Networking is a way of letting people know not only that you are available for work but also:

- the sort of work that you do

- the kind of skills that you have

- your perspective on employment.

When you start networking your first aim isn't just to get a job, but to make the person that you are talking to feel relaxed and interested in you. Here are some tips.

- Always introduce yourself in a very positive and clear way. This may sound obvious, but all too often in these situations we find ourselves hesitating, shuffling from foot to foot, not clearly saying who we are.

- Try to make eye contact. Don't be threatening, but use it as a linking tool.

- Ask them direct questions; what, where, when, how and why? People enjoy talking about themselves so make them feel that they are being listened to.

- Be sure that you do listen, rather than just thinking about your reply or your next question.

- Don't let your eyes wander elsewhere; it's a tell-tale sign that you aren't really interested. People remember and appreciate a good listener.

- Remember some aspect of what they are talking about, so that you can ask them about it when you next speak to them. It shows that you took a genuine interest in what they were saying and gives you a more personal link into your meeting with them, rather than having to remind them who you are. People are impressed when someone takes the trouble to recall something about them, however trivial.

- Don't give your selling pitch about yourself the first time you meet someone, as this can be a complete turn-off. You don't want to come across as being too pushy.

- You need to build a relationship and develop a sense of what's in it for the other person, such as what they are looking for and what the needs of their company are.

- Don't switch off on someone the moment that you realise that they probably aren't of any use to you; after all networking is all about layers, and they just might know someone who could be a potential contact.

- Talking through your employment needs helps you to understand what it is that you're looking for, builds your confidence and helps you to perfect a technique of selling yourself, which you can carry through to your CV and an interview.

If you are self-employed and either running your own business or working on short contracts, your networking should be pitched slightly differently. Think about the following:

- Target people who would use you or your product by contacting identified buyers or companies whose products are similar to yours. Business directories are very useful for this and are available at your local reference library.

- Use the same networking skills, always developing and looking after your contacts.

- When you think it is appropriate, ask your contact if they know any of the senior people within any of the companies that you have targeted and whether they can refer you to any of these personally.

- What you're looking for is the name of an appropriate person to write to, or phone, someone who is actually in the position of buying or hiring, or is close to a person in this position, rather than you just cold calling.

- At a meeting it helps to break the ice if you mention the name of your mutual contact – that's if they've given you the OK to do so.

Try never to end a networking meeting without asking for more contacts. In other words, never stop networking. When you've moved on, remember always to keep your original contact involved with your progress, especially with the companies or individuals that they suggested, because since your meeting they may have other ideas that would be helpful to you.

Networking Dos and Don'ts

Dos

If a contact passes you on to someone they know, here's what you should do:

- Always report back to them and tell them that you followed up their leads.

- Tell them what happened, even if it wasn't anything earth shattering and you didn't get a job out of it. It's a way of showing that you respect their advice, that you are keen and that you aren't wasting their time. Who knows, they may have some other ideas if that one didn't work out.

- Most people like to have some positive feedback about what happened to you with one of their contacts. They'll be so flattered and surprised that you did as they suggested, as so many people don't, that they will usually be willing to put on their thinking hats and come up with someone else. This will also help to fix you firmly in their mind when someone else asks if they know of anyone with your skills and expertise.

- A networking contact can help to sell you to an organisation by 'putting a good word in for you', in other words recommending you. For example, it may be something along the lines of them saying to your potential future employer that despite your age, they ought to give you an interview.

- Your contacts may also be in a position to give you information from other employment sources that would not otherwise be available to you. All this is widening your network and the more people you contact the more chance you have of finding employment.

Don'ts

You will find that the majority of people like to help and will feel flattered when they are asked for advice:

• But don't make other people feel responsible for getting you a job. The one basic networking rule, however tempting it may be and however desperate you may feel, is not to ask a friend if they can give you or get you a job. It is guaranteed to ruin any relationship, because it immediately makes the other person feel responsible for you. They feel guilty if they are unable to fulfil your request and anger because you made them feel either of the above.

Instead just ask for their advice and guidance. You know how you would respond if someone asked you. Ask them who they know and this will make your network even wider, moving you on to another layer of contacts.

THE INTERNET AS A JOB-FINDING TOOL

In order to advertise your skills on the Internet you have to pay an Internet Service Provider a monthly subscription to get on-line. There are now ISPs who will get you on to the Internet for free (see Useful Information for further details). In the UK there are around thirty different providers to choose from. Once you have an Internet provider your computer is connected to others around the world via a telephone line and you can then advertise your interests and skills on the Internet, hoping that people with the same interests and skills will contact you.

Homepages are very smart Internet bulletin boards which are supplied by your Internet provider. It's very common to find CVs on home pages. Demon, for example, which is one of the largest Internet providers in the UK, currently has 165,000 CVs on it. You can either buy a computer programme which will help you to make a very simple homepage or you can pay for a specialist to design one for you, but this can be very expensive. Your CV or any other information that you put on your home-page, will stay there for as long as you want. In order to find your CV people would just have to key in the word that describes your area of skills and your homepage will come up with your details.

The purpose of putting your CV on your homepage is that it

will be seen by someone who is in the position of being able to offer you a job. This method of job searching is similar to putting up a card with information about yourself on it on the bulletin board of a supermarket, hoping that someone will see it. The downside is that it doesn't allow you to target or tailor your CV to a particular employer's needs, but what it does do very successfully is give you an insight into what is on offer by allowing you to see other CVs and job advertisements from all over the world. This can be very useful if you're trying to make a career change, or you are considering working abroad.

Large companies have homepages which can be very eye catching, similar to the cover of a book, with an index inside and pages of information about themselves, the job vacancies they have available and the services they offer. Looking at the job vacancies will give you an idea of what jobs are available. There will usually be a contact number for further information and job specifications. If a certain job interests you then you can e-mail your CV and ask for further job details.

Most large employment agencies have a web page with a standard CV questionnaire on it. Complete the basic form adding additional information about yourself. Job agencies keep CVs on file until they have an employer they can match you with. Some job agency web pages also give CV and interview advice.

Companies and large organisations now sift through CVs by using software that picks out key words which are relevant to the skills and personality types that they are looking for. In order for your CV to pass this software test you should use positive words such as: qualified, experienced, trained, administered, initiated, managed, proficient, resourceful, developed, designed, capable and profitable. For your personal skills use words such as: mediating between people, planning agendas, corresponding with customers, coaching individuals, running meetings, drafting reports, supervising staff, motivating others and serving the public.

The Internet is another way of widening your circle of potential employers or having access to potential jobs in a very short time. It offers you more or less the world, which is especially helpful if you're thinking about working abroad. Certainly there are many people out there using the Internet. Since 1996 the number of Internet users has risen by nearly 300 per cent.

Despite receiving around 5,000 hits a day, one employment agency which runs a large IT job site on the Internet, has held back from charging its clients for its promotion of jobs on the Web because they see it as a value-added service, while their clients still prefer the traditional ways of promoting jobs.

Recruiters are also finding difficulties with the openness of the Internet. Anyone, anywhere in the world has access to the information on it and there isn't much you can do to prevent that. Therefore employers advertising job vacancies have found they are receiving applications from all over the world. The problem with this isn't that those applying may not be suitable for the job, or that they aren't more than willing to move to the UK, but it can unleash legal issues involving work permits.

One recruitment site offers a regional salary calculator that enables you to select the region in which you want to work and discover the comparative salaries. For example, a job advertised in Devon has a salary of £20,000, while the same job in Buckinghamshire would pay a salary of £26,316. One US organisation on the Internet offers complete relocating information across the the states, giving regional salary differences, local schools and home finding help (see Chapter 13).

Newsgroups

Newsgroups can be another useful tool in your job search. Through a newsgroup you can contact people by simply sending a letter which contains your e-mail address, via your computer. Once on the Internet the letter will find the relevant newsgroup that interests you. There are 30,000 newsgroups across Europe, the US and Australia and some advertise jobs, but they tend to be in areas of employment that require IT skills and be in large computer based organisations. You can also contact employers by putting up a newsgroup bulletin about yourself, but the downside of this is that it puts you in competition with the world, which can be overwhelming and newsgroup messages aren't permanent; they are only displayed for around a month.

Data Protection

When you put your CV or information about yourself or your business on the Internet, it becomes the property of the world. Nothing can stop anyone, anywhere from reading it. The upside of this is that it makes you accessible to the world, and the result could be that your CV may attract employers from anywhere. If it's the world that you're interested in, because you want to work abroad for example, then this can be very useful, but the downside is that it exposes information about you that anyone can copy or misuse.

We all have the right to know what is recorded about us by computers and this is controlled by the Data Protection Act 1984, which set up the Data Protection Register. This only covers the UK. Anyone who keeps information about living people who can be identified has to have a licence to do so. The register is open for public inspection.

Internet access providers are organisations that are likely to hold personal data about their customers for running their business such as billing clients, controlling access and so on. They have their own code of practice set up by the Internet Service Providers Association (ISPA), which requires members to state in their application forms that data may be used for regulatory purposes.

Organisations that keep records on computer must comply with the Data Protection Principles as set out in the Act. These are:

- records must be obtained and used fairly and lawfully

- information must be adequate, relevant and not excessive

- data must not be kept for longer than is necessary

- individuals must be allowed to check the data and have errors corrected or removed.

There are simple ways that you can protect yourself, such as:

- if you are putting your CV on the Internet you should only give your e-mail address, not your home or business address

- do not give out any personal details about yourself or your business, or details which you do not want everyone to know. Give a broad-brush outline of your working career and qualifications, adding that if any further information is required it will be available either by private correspondence or at an interview

- if an organisation, such as an employment agency, wants to put your CV on the Internet, they have to ask you for your permission.

WHEN NO ONE EMPLOYS YOU

'I've been for loads of interviews and sent out hundreds of CVs and I haven't been offered anything. It's been a waste of time.' You've all heard it, maybe even some of you have said it. When you're trying to find a job, getting a nil response isn't a waste of time. It's telling you that either you're going about your job search the wrong way or you are aiming at the wrong target. Either way you've got to reassess.

Finding employment isn't any longer just a matter of waiting for the phone to ring or calling up some old contacts from way back when and hoping that, along with what you consider to be a brilliant CV and a sure-fire interview technique, you'll crack it. That was then, and this is now. Companies have realised that in the competitive world economy as it now stands, one of the things success depends on is highly skilled employees. This is why they are investing substantial amounts of time, money and expertise in making sure they choose the right person for the right job. What you have to make sure is that you are that person, and that the job you are looking for is the one that fits your CV and your skills.

When you are looking for employment you must use all the job-finding tools that are available to you. What we have looked at in this chapter is the range of them, how to make the best use of them and how they can work for you. There are the tried and tested methods of job finding, such as making the best use of your CV right through to using job recruitment sites on the Internet and handling an interview.

If it's a new career path that you're looking at, then be thorough with your skills audit. You need to be sure that you are looking for employment in an area that interests you, that you have skills and talents you can build on and are transferable, and that it is an area of employment with a future.

Keep in mind the fact that job searching is probably something that you are all going to have to do every few years, so you need to get skilled at it. Never turn down any re-training opportunities, especially if your employer is willing to pay. However irrelevant they may seem to you now, you have no idea where your employment path will take you. Continue to build on your networking, you never know when you might need it. You know the importance of targeting employers, of making sure that your CV is doing the best selling job it possibly can for you and that when you finally get that interview you are prepared for every aspect of it and from the moment you walk into the room you are selling yourself and your skills.

CHAPTER 10

Dealing with Crisis

Many elements of employment are changing. Boundaries have moved, forcing us to reflect not only on our belief in our work, but our ability to obtain it and remain in it. It means we have to re-evaluate the ways in which we confront our ambitions and our abilities, often with little time for preparation and sometimes with one foot firmly planted in the past. This can make us feel that we have no control over our future which can be highly stressful, leaving us anxious and depressed. This is why stress, in all its many forms, is now being recognised as a problem, and the reason why there are times when we all suffer from being unable to function at our best.

Redundancy and the new technology are just two of the key stress factors at work. They can cause highly confident skilled workers to become depressed and insecure.

ANDREW, a successful merchant banker in the 1980s, watched the organisation that he worked for slimming down because of the new technology and laying off employees in all areas of the business. 'The stress levels were terrible because you didn't have any control over what was happening. They didn't fire fifty of us in one hit; it was gradual, spread out over a few weeks. You just knew heads were on the block, but I didn't think one of them was mine, because I'd brought business into the bank. Funnily enough when it was my turn to be dumped my initial reaction was relief. It was only later I felt angry, then I wanted to screw them, then I started to worry about how my family and I would survive. Months later the terrible depression took over and I found life very difficult.' It took Andrew a year and some counselling before he was able to start positively looking for work, 'I couldn't function, I felt as if my very reason for being had been taken from me. Without a job I felt as if I didn't exist.' Andrew took several IT courses and found a new job working abroad for another banking organisation.

The workplace has become highly stressful. If you're working in it, then you know it, because you're there wrestling with the fast-changing new technology, probably a slimmed down workforce and employers who are continually looking at the bottom line, pushing you to work harder and longer, and not to complain. If you're unemployed, then you know about the stress of job finding and making a career move.

GOOD STRESS, BAD STRESS

The word stress is derived from the Latin *stringere*, meaning to pull tight, and was originally used to describe hardship or affliction. Now stress is how we describe the mind and the body's response to pressure. There are many reasons for the increase in the levels of stress at work, from downsizing and information overload to survivors' syndrome, and, however hard we try to avoid it, it seems that we all have the ability to be victims of stress at one time or another. There will always be some situations, either at home or at work, which will induce pessimism, anxiety and often sheer panic in the most secure of us.

Most of us can handle a certain amount of stress in our lives; in fact some of us function better with additional pressures, moving us forward and inducing us to produce our best achievements. The problems arise when demand exceeds our resources for coping, such as when we are working long hours or our job feels insecure and there are a lot of changes within the workforce, and we start to feel as if we no longer have any control over our lives. This can be the biggest stress trigger.

It was not until the Second World War that stress began to be taken seriously by scientists. Long hours in munitions factories took their toll on health, reflected in absenteeism, and increased drinking and smoking. During the 1950s and 1960s the rise in heart disease in men was identified and, since they made up the bulk of the workforce, it was suggested that stress was a factor. Wider recognition came with a study in the 1960s that showed a direct link between ambition, aggressiveness, hostility and heart disease. The work remains controversial, but investigations into the link between stress and illness continue.

Stress and Downsizing

A recent report from Finland found that downsizing can lead to increased job insecurity, changes in the nature of work and the working environment, and a deterioration in the relationship between management and employees. Clinical research on the effects of job insecurity showed that the threat of redundancy can result in anxiety, depression, burnout, poor self-reported health status, poor quality of sleep, and an increased rate of absenteeism because of ill health and heart disease. These symptoms were especially noticeable among people over the age of forty-four and those in workplaces with a high proportion of older employees.

Even managers, who at one time were thought to have control over their employment and only suffered low levels of stress, are now suffering from the stress of rapid change. They say that their morale is low, they are kept in the dark by their seniors and suffer from constant insecurity about their jobs. Thirty-eight per cent of workers in the UK feel that their organisation has become a worse place to work in the last twelve months, while over half either felt, or were made to feel guilty about taking time off even when they were ill.

Certainly experts are agreed that downsizing has caused a lot of the problems which are worse than the 1980s enterprise era when the stress was self-induced. Now the changes are more stressful because they are not within our control.

Less Control, More Stress

It isn't only those in management and those who work with the new information technology who are suffering from stress; some of the most stressful jobs are those where the person doing the work has the least control, least variety and little or no opportunity to develop or use their skills.

This was highlighted in a recent British study of the Civil Service, where it was found that people in the lowest grades are three times more likely to die over a ten-year period than senior administrators, and that they have six times more sick leave. The three classic risk factors for heart disease – cholesterol levels, blood pressure and smoking – accounted for only a third of the different rates of heart disease that were found. There was strong evidence that people at the bottom of the hierarchy produce higher levels of the stress hormone called cortisol and this can cause widespread biological damage in the long term, including heart disease and diabetes. Stress over long periods also harms the immune system, which can in turn contribute to higher levels of cancer and infectious diseases. You should be aware that it isn't just the high powered high profile jobs that are stressful, but those jobs where you have little power but lots of responsibility can create stress.

If you are in that type of situation make sure that you learn how to recognise and handle your stress levels, that you have interests outside of work that help you to unwind and take your mind completely off your job – hobby isn't a dirty word, it can be a lifesaver. Learn to delegate and pass work on to those who have more authority than you do. If this isn't possible then you should discuss with your employer or trade union ways in which the chain of command can be restructured or ways in which you can be given more authority to deal with situations directly involved in your area of employment.

Stress Symptoms

Dr Hans Seyle, an Austrian physiologist, author of *Stress Without Distress*, says that it is not stress that is harmful – it is *dis*tress.

Distress occurs when emotional stress is prolonged and not dealt with in a positive way. The physical and emotional state that results from distress can lead to illness.

We are all aware of the levels of stress that we are having to deal with. Technology has brought the world to our doorstep and downsizing has taken job insecurity through the ceiling. No wonder we are stressed out and it's having an effect on our work performance, our home lives and our relationships.

Some of the symptoms of stress are chronic fatigue, inertia, loss of interest in appearance, low tolerance levels, snapping at everyone, feeling that nothing is fun, depression, panic attacks, drinking too much alcohol, excessive smoking, nail-biting, crying easily over 'nothing', having difficulty concentrating or making decisions, suffering from memory lapses, inefficiency, anxiety, hypochondria, phobias and obsessions.

Information Fatigue

Do you ever feel bombarded by information? That you just must answer those faxes, e-mails and answer machine messages immediately and surf the net reading through hundreds of pages of information that you don't necessarily need? With the new technology it's easy to find yourself caught up in information overload and the stress that it creates. The truth is that we don't just *feel* we are being inundated with information, we are. For example, any weekday edition of the *New York Times* contains more information than the average person living in seventeenth-century Britain would have come across in their entire lifetime. More information has been produced in the past thirty years than in the past five millenniums. No wonder we're finding it exhausting.

Company psychologists say that about half of us are stressed out and anxious about being plagued daily by information produced by the explosion in modern communications. This feeling of overload can affect our home lives, our personal relationships and is the reason why many of us have to work late or take work home. There's simply too much to choose from and too many communications to reply to. The end result is that we are more likely to make incorrect decisions, suffer from headaches, extreme tiredness, irritability, forgetfulness, loss of concentration, disturbed sleep, anxiety and 'computer rage' – literally hitting the PC. As the condition worsens, you will suffer increased levels of general illness.

Handling Information Overload

What can you do? Modern technology and the deluge of information that it brings isn't going to go away. If anything the new technology of the future will take us even further into information city. You have to control it for the sake of your own stress levels and quality of life. In order to do this you should:

- If possible, and consider this as a serious option, throw away your mobile phone or limit the number of people who can contact you on your mobile phone.

- Limit the time you spend surfing the net.

- Only answer a maximum of ten e-mails a day.

- When surfing the net for information learn to only read what you need.

- Remember this technology is a working tool and is there to relieve pressures on your workload, not add to them.

- Learn to scan or speed read.

- Learn to prioritise, and only answer or deal with what is truly important or urgent.

In order to lighten the overload, one US company has set up 'knowledge centres'. This is where information is brought together and filtered, in order to pull out the relevant details. There is no reason why you can't do the same thing, simply by being subjective and sifting out the dead wood of information, in other words by creating your own 'knowledge centre' pulling out the information that you need and discarding the rest, or putting it on the back burner.

E-mails and faxes

There is no need to respond immediately to all faxes, as most of them are no more urgent than a letter you would receive the next day in the post. Ignore the fact that all faxes these days are called 'urgent'. Prioritise what is truly 'urgent' to you. Forget the buzz that you perhaps once got from believing that being contacted means being wanted.

If you have a fax machine at home make a rule of not looking at it after a certain time, the time that you need for yourself, be it half an hour in the middle of each day, or at a certain time in the morning and evening.

Limit the time that you spend surfing the Net. A survey commissioned by Reuters Business Information found that people using the Internet are more likely to feel depressed and lonely. By the end of the study the researchers found that one hour a week on the Internet led to an average increase of 1 per cent on the depression scale, a loss of 2.7 members of the subject's social circle and an increase of 0.4 per cent on the so-called lonely scale.

Don't automatically set up your lap-top the moment you sit down in a plane or train. Rationalise whether or not you truly need to do that work at that time or only for part of that time. The journey may be better spent winding down, reading relevant paper documents, mulling over business or private thoughts.

Chronic Fatigue

This is an alternative physical expression of stress, in which the 'flight or fight' instinct is replaced by extreme exhaustion. At least a third of us suffer from this constant weariness and lack of energy at some time in our lives. If possible you should try to take as much rest as you can. Try to take an annual holiday, even if you just stay at home and rest. Make sure that you relax at weekends and unwind at the end of the day. No one is indispensable. If there is a panic situation at work, or if you work in a seasonal job, try to return to your usual work pattern when it's over. If none of this is possible it may be more beneficial for your health to work part time or job share. Talk to your employer to see if this is possible (and see Chapter 6 of this book for alternative ways of working).

Depression

According to a survey carried out by the Samaritans there is significant stigma attached to stress and depression. Stress sufferers have a prevailing fear of losing their jobs, as one interviewee said, 'You wouldn't be able to get promoted at work if you said you were depressed' and another added, 'There is an unwritten rule that you don't bring your problems to work.'

The Samaritans say that if you know or work with anyone who is depressed you should:

- offer emotional support

- encourage them to talk about their feelings – reassure them that your conversation is completely confidential

- understand that they often have low self-esteem, and feel ashamed and guilty that they are finding it difficult to cope. It's important not to pass judgement or offer solutions, however tempting it can be, just listening is more valuable.

The Cost of Stress

Stress and stress-related illnesses have become the second most frequent cause of absenteeism at work, after the common cold. The result is that stress in the UK is now costing businesses £7 billion a year, once sick pay, missed deadlines and poor performance are taken into account. It's also costing the taxpayer heavily because those working in the public sector – in schools, social services and the health service – appear to take even more time off to recover from the results of stress compared to those employed in privately run companies. Even the courts are becoming involved. Local authorities are being hit for compensation claims for causing stress, in the form of legal action. In economic terms the CBI puts the total cost of mental health and stress problems at £5 billion a year; this is equal to industry's total annual losses through theft and many, many times the cost of strike.

Working long hours isn't helping. Professor Cary Cooper, a psychologist specialising in organisational management, says that workers in the UK work the longest average week in the EU, with 16 per cent working more than forty-eight hours a week, and 50 per cent saying that they come home at the end of the working day feeling totally exhausted. It's thought that we are motivated to work such long hours out of fear and belief that we can only keep our jobs if we show even more commitment to our employers. The other reason is that many of us are having to work longer hours in order to earn the money we need. Work in itself has become highly stressful, since after downsizing and a shrinking workforce many of us are expected to do the job that was previously done by our colleagues, as well as doing our own.

The rest of this chapter is going to help you to recognise stress in all its different forms, and find positive ways of dealing with it so that it doesn't affect your ability to work. Taking a longer view of things it tells you simple ways in which you can de-stress your life in order to avoid burnout.

Controlling Stress

Mobile phones, which at one time were a status symbol, are today one of the biggest stressors simply because users are accessible every minute of every day. In Cantonese the translation of mobile phone literally means 'little big brother'. If a company in Hong Kong wants to show you that you are a trusted and valued employee, they no longer give you a mobile phone. They don't feel they have to be a 'big brother' to you. It is hoped that employers around the world will follow their lead. Meanwhile, mobile phones continue to interrupt lunches, meetings and calm times.

It is important to find a few quiet moments to mull over the day's events, make internal decisions that will later affect our outer ones, study strategies and weigh up the pros and cons of business situations. These are often the times when the best and most important work practices are put in place. They are also the times when we can calm ourselves in whichever way works best for us.

If there are work reasons why you aren't able to get rid of your mobile phone, make a start by remembering where the 'off' button is. Give out your phone number to as few people as possible. Let the answerphone take the strain. Only respond to the messages on your answer machine that you consider to be urgent – these are usually very few. Only reply to a certain number, no more than five; the others you can reply to in order of importance later. Remember, you are getting rid of the dead wood of information. Give yourself value time, to unwind, to de-tune, to deal with the information that you already have.

Stress Relief

Once you have pin-pointed your symptoms, there are many ways of relieving stress. But before you seek outside help, try to find the cause of your stress. In order to do this be sensitive to your stress triggers. Be a stress detective. When you feel under stress work out when it started. You may be causing the stress yourself by over-reacting, in which case analyse why and then take positive moves to change the source of the problem. You may find it easier to do this when you are not actually under stress, but sitting quietly alone and can play back in your mind the stressful events. If you have a friend or partner ask them, as often people on the outside who know us well can see the way we react more than we ourselves can. Try simple solutions such as regularly walking, jogging or playing team sports. Make sure you are getting enough sleep and eating properly. Remember weekends really are time off, so try not to think about work or whatever is causing you to feel stressed. Don't take drugs or drink too much alcohol; they only bring temporary relief and the next day the stress is still there. Don't forget to laugh.

There are a number of alternative therapies that help with stress. These include osteopathy, acupuncture, homeopathy, herbalism, aromatherapy, reflexology, hypnotherapy, yoga, physiotherapy, biofeedback (learning to recognise the body's responses to stress and learning how to control them), the Alexander technique (concerned with posture and relaxation, freeing the body from tension) and cognitive behaviour therapy (which teaches you how to recognise the automatic negative thoughts that flash into your brain and then dispute them by focusing on contrary evidence and offering more positive explanations to the self-attacking ones). For further information on any of these therapies there are many books available or you can write to the relevant organisations (see Part 4).

Self-assertiveness

A good way of combating stress is learning to be self-assertive rather than aggressive – to get even, not get mad. You can practise this by focusing on what it is you want from a situation, not floundering around in frustration when you don't get it.

Women were culturally encouraged not to be very assertive, as society saw this as male behaviour. However, this is gradually changing and slowly women are becoming more assertive, seeing that their needs are met and their voice is heard. In a male-dominated workplace, some men are still worried by assertive women and encourage women to fall back on the stereotype behaviour of flirting and cajoling to get what they want. Men generally tend to have a distorted idea of assertiveness and see it as bullying, using physical violence, language that promotes fear and publicly embarrassing others.

The true meaning of assertiveness is communicating openly, honestly, directly and making sure that your needs are met and your voice is heard. For people who find this difficult, assertiveness training can be extremely beneficial. Once it has been learnt, and you are shown different and more appropriate ways of handling situations, both your own anger and other people's, the result is higher self-esteem, more self-confidence and less anxiety. You can learn to take responsibility for yourself and your own needs. Assertiveness training involves learning and practising new skills. It will show you how to become aware of what you are saying and stop using qualifying or apologetic language. You will see assertiveness as improved self-esteem and self-worth, not as aggression, insubordination and, for women, unfeminine. Above all you will see that being assertive can also win you respect.

Self-assertion training courses are available from most adult education authorities (see Part 4 for addresses and further details).

Exercise

General exercise, apart from keeping us in good shape, is also good for stress relief. Often our bodies want to take physical action to combat stress, in the flight or fight instinct, and without exercise mental tensions tend to build up. Stress levels are lower in fit people. Inactive students were put on an aerobic programme of brisk walking or jogging for forty minutes three times a week, and after fourteen weeks they were given a series of unsolvable problems and told that their results would be critical for their academic career. After being told this those who exercised had lower blood pressure and lower levels of anxiety and muscle tension than the non-exercisers. Exercise can also help to lift your depression and give you a more optimistic outlook.

There is a whole range of exercise techniques available, but you don't have to punish yourself. The harder you push yourself at the beginning the more likely you are to quit. Researchers have found that relatively gentle exercise combined with relaxation techniques – such as listening to relaxation tapes while walking – showed improved fitness, reduced anxiety and enhanced mood.

Before starting any exercise regime you should check with your doctor.

Quick-Fix Stress Busters

• Learn to say no.

• Make a list, daily or weekly, of things you have to do. Base it on reality – only include tasks you know you are able to achieve. Don't make your list too long or you won't complete it and then you will feel you have failed.

- Write down your thoughts and feelings for no one's eyes but your own. It will help you to put them in perspective and then let them go.

- Unplug your phone or put on your answer machine when you are lying in the bath, eating, meditating, being still, reading, doing your hair – however you unwind in your own time.

- Laugh – remember your smile muscles.

- Don't deal with other people's problems, you'll start to resent them.

- Don't rely on your memory, it's got enough to deal with, so write yourself reminders.

- Make sure you get enough sleep.

- Say 'no' to extra projects that you don't have the energy for.

- Do one thing at a time.

- Prioritise.

- Learn to time manage. If you're beating the clock ask yourself if you really need to do something.

- Delegate, even if it's only the ironing.

- Don't ignore opening your mail.

- Make duplicate sets of keys and photocopy your address books and credit cards so that it won't cause an emergency if you lose them.

- Don't use food, drugs, alcohol or misplaced anger as stress relievers.

- Do some kind of exercise – power walking, jogging, aerobics, cycling.

- Cut up your credit cards. Debt is highly stressful.

- Learn to be more assertive.

SURVIVORS' SYNDROME

SINCE DOWNSIZING Tony is the longest-serving commercial sales person left in the company where he works. Now one person is doing a job that was previously done by three. Tony is one of these. 'I thought of myself as a super sales and marketing man, now I suddenly find I'm in charge of twenty-eight guys, plant managers, engineers and process operators, and although I've been on some training courses I don't feel I'm trained to do the extra work.'

'But what's the point in complaining, they'll just tell me if I don't like it I can go elsewhere. When they laid off the first lot of people, they got rid of them all in two days. This time they've been gentler. They asked for volunteers but not enough people came forward. That's when they started calling people in to fire them. We all sat around in stunned silence. Just waiting to see if we were called. I was lucky, I'd been told that I was personally safe. But I was shocked that they effectively got rid of everyone in one fell swoop. The ones who were fired were shocked too, then they were angry. I felt guilty that I'd survived. Others felt frightened that it would be them next. Lots of workers now go home and get pissed every night. For some time before and after the firings I couldn't sleep. I'd wake up in the night, worried about what was going to happen to us, to my family and then there's the continual guilt, that I'm still in a job and a lot of my colleagues were just got rid of because the company needed to make cuts. There's no loyalty left. They've saved money but they've destroyed the intercommunication in the company. In the old days we worked as teams, now there's no one left. If I got fired tomorrow it would be a sort of relief. Nothing can be as bad as working like this. I don't know what I'd do, but I don't care – work as a labourer, anything would be better than this mixture of anger, guilt and fear.'

Tony is just one of the 57 per cent of employees in the UK who have seen colleagues laid off in the last five years leaving those left behind experiencing guilt and fear as part of 'survivors' syndrome', a term coined by Professor Cary Cooper, a psychologist at the University of Manchester specialising in stress and organisational management. Some organisations are starting to look at the stress suffered, not only by those workers who have lost their jobs, but more importantly for the company the anxiety and insecurity of the workers who are left behind and will have to carry the additional workload.

Employers may have thought that workers who have kept their jobs will be relieved and happy, when in fact they tend to be even more worried that it'll be their turn next. Frequently employees work longer hours than they are contracted to do and return home exhausted. Many psychologists believe this is out of fear, because workers think that they must show even more commitment to the company or it'll be their turn next. The truth is that they tend to be so exhausted that they are probably the people who'll start making the mistakes.

CERTAINLY JOHN, who works in corporate PR and is in his late forties, reflects this. He works an average sixty-six hours a week and travels 130,000 miles a year. He's only taken one week's holiday in the last twelve months and was recently told by his boss that if he valued his job he would have to put in some more hours. John thinks that his situation has become worse since the company downsized, causing his work load to dramatically increase. He is starting to feel that because of the hours he's now expected to work he isn't able to put in his best effort. People in John's position are not unionised and therefore don't have an outside complaints procedure. They are working longer hours with a heavier work load and not complaining because they are frightened that if they do they risk losing their job.

Even the self-employed are not immune from this exhaustion and the continual fear of losing clients if they don't keep up the work load.

GILLIAN, a self-employed freelance graphic artist, gave up her job when she realised she was working more than fifty hours a week and had no life outside of her work. She thought going freelance would give her some control over her life and she might even have time for socialising. Instead, she finds that she's working seven days a week and she can't recall the last time she and her husband went out together.

As more and more people have become self-employed, often after being made redundant, the competition for clients and customers is high. The result is that the self-employed are now working harder and putting in longer hours in order to stay in business. For a lot of people the point of going self-employed was to be able to have more control over their working hours and spend more time with their family: this option now hardly exists. As a self-employed accountant said, 'There's no let up, I've ended up working seven Mondays.'

In two-thirds of British families both partners work. Professor Cooper believes that unless employers start to accept that their staff have a life outside of their job, the impact of parents being absent from their families will be catastrophic. 'The old work ethos of long hours may have worked when wives stayed at home,' says Cooper, 'but the long-term effects of presentee-ism on families where both partners work will be ill health and less effective performance when they do work.' He believes that in the future more work will be contracted out, so that even those of us who are self-employed will be suffering exhaustion from the severe pressure caused by working long hours.

Insecurity and fear is how a lot of people describe their feelings after a wave of redundancies. Those left often decide to adopt a sort of to-hell-with-this-company attitude which not only reflects on productivity and performance but also throws loyalty out of the window. As one employer put it, 'If we're not careful we're going to end up with a labour force of over-timid zombies and conflicts being forced underground, left there to fester like so many untreated wounds in the corporate soul.'

Avoiding Survivors' Syndrome

The symptoms of survivors' syndrome have to be recognised and acknowledged by your employers. They have to be reminded of how important and valuable the general morale of their work force is, especially after redundancies, because their organisation is going to depend on you to keep it going. You can help to make your employers become more aware by using the various channels of communication that are open to you such as:

- A working or trade association, ie the CBI, that would cover your particular area of business.

- Your trade union.

- Your personnel department.

- Your immediate line manager.

- Your work bulletin board, staff newsletter and other means of internal communications.

You may feel that you are totally powerless and are frightened that in speaking out you are in danger of losing your job. But you don't have to discuss this face to face, you can write a memo or go through your trade union or trade association.

The more your employers realise the effects, in terms of cost, production loss and company loyalty that survivors' syndrome has on their business, the more willing they will be to listen to your suggestions. You should be asking to set in place for employees: counselling, two-way forms of communication, re-training and greater transparency so that everyone is aware of future business plans, progress and problems. For example, a Japanese consumer-products company has an internal information network which allows everybody to find out anything and everything to do with the company. The more of that type of information that is available to the entire organisation the less of a shock and more understanding there is if the situation worsens forcing cuts in the workforce.

The aim is that if redundancies are going to happen, you should all have access to the following:

- A full explanation of the situation – not just those who are going to be made redundant, but everyone in the company.

- The policy and practice that the company has regarding:

  – selection

  – re-training

  – compensation

  – counselling and other support.

- Individual sessions should be given offering reassurance as to the importance of each person in the organisation, their job security and their employment prospects.

- Counselling will also help to relieve feelings of guilt and anxiety, with emotional debriefing and on-going support.

Any trade unions or elected employee representatives should be included in these discussions.

If you have a friend or partner who is suffering from survivors' syndrome, you should:

- not tell them to pull themselves together

- allow them time to express their own individual fears

- listen

- suggest that they should see their doctor and ask for counselling

- encourage them to avoid alcohol and drugs as they only bring temporary relief.

LOOK OUT! THERE'S A BULLY ABOUT

In these times of downsizing and job insecurity it takes a lot of courage to stand up to a bullying boss. Downsizing and the pressure it puts on decreasing staff – with increasing workloads – is one of the reasons why bullying at work is on the increase. Remember that people bully because they can get away with it, so one of the ways to stop it quickly is to report it. One senior business lecturer who has carried out several surveys on the subject believes that only a small percentage of bullying bosses are motivated by sadistic tendencies and victims have two common hopes – that the bullying will stop and they will be able to remain in their jobs. It is estimated that 40 million working days are lost through bullying, that's 160 times more than are lost through strikes.

Bullying at work has at last come out of the closet and is now being recognised as a form of employment humiliation. Research shows that managers are particularly adept at humiliating employees publicly or intimidating them in an attempt to drive them harder. Those who have survived downsizing, and are already suffering from fear and guilt, are highly vulnerable to the office bully, who senses that they won't complain, for fear of being in the next wave of layoffs.

Andrea Adams, author of a book on bullying at work, told a union conference in 1994 'Bullying is the most stressful, destructive, humiliating and financially undermining factor in the UK employment scene. It is the persistent demeaning and downgrading of human beings. Bullies make cruel and vindictive attacks on the personal or professional ability of their victims who are often reduced to the state of frightened children, vomiting on their way to work, taking extensive sick leave, sometimes for many months, and hiding in the toilets to avoid their tormentors.'

Whatever techniques you choose to stop the bullying, and there are many, at the end of the day the problem is that if someone has decided that they are going to destroy your self-esteem then it's going to be difficult to stop them simply by using a psychological approach. You have to go to whoever deals with this type of behaviour at your workplace. If there isn't structure in place to deal with it, then you have to talk openly with your colleagues about the arrangements to put one in place. If you have a trade union then you should involve them. If you have any other type of trade organisation, you should contact them. Bullies don't like being in the limelight.

Certainly several employers, banks, universities, the Royal Mail and colleges have introduced bullying policies. The Benefits Agency and the Contributions Agency have already agreed procedures on bullying and unions have a bullying advice list for employers.

If bullying is a problem in your workplace:

- make sure that your employer understands the importance of having a bullying procedure

- prepare a procedure for reporting, recording and dealing with incidents

- ask for access to trained counsellors

- make sure that your confidentiality is respected

- don't be afraid to report it right from the start, before it gets established

- stand up for yourself, it will give you a great feeling of potential and freedom

- tell everyone – don't keep it a secret – share your problem with your family and friends

- keep a record or diary of the bullying, as you may need it if there is an enquiry

- inform the police if it becomes physical or physically threatening

- tell your union or work representative right from the start

- tell your doctor or medical staff where you work, as you may need their support if it affects your health.

There isn't an easy, quick-fix answer to bullying, but the main message is don't be afraid to report it, the earlier the better, before it gets established.

Conclusion

As we have seen in this chapter stress manifests itself in many different ways, and there are an assortment of ways of dealing with it. Often we can de-stress our working lives by using quick-fix stress busters, while at other times we may need outside professional help. We also have to realise that the new techno-logy is a tool that's meant to be there to make our work easier and less stressful. Once we have learnt how to use it, then just as importantly we must learn to control our use of it. There may be no escape from some amount of stress in our working lives, but we must and can learn to handle it.

PART 4

Useful Information

CHAPTER 11

Golden Keys

In this book we have looked at the changing face of employment and the knock-on effect these changes are having on all of us. Without getting into crystal ball gazing we know the changes both now and in the future will mean:

- You will have multiple employers which will bring interesting and varied employment.

- The ageing population will need care which will open up new job opportunities.

- A lot of older people will have surplus income which will bring new growth areas of employment.

- The higher your skills the better chance you have of finding work.

- IT specialist skills will be in demand and highly paid.

- Leisure and service industries will grow.

- You will have to recharge your re-training batteries every few years.

- You will become more highly skilled and more adaptable.

- Your everyday life and your employment will blend into one as more of you work from home, telecommute, work part time and become self-employed.

- Teleworking will become a vital part of business and open up huge employment opportunities especially in areas where they were thin on the ground.

- You will have the chance to be more assertive, fine tuning your interview and networking techniques.

- Gaining more skills and qualifications in order to change careers will be easier because technology will make distance learning more instantly available.

- Numeracy, record keeping, quality monitoring, an understanding of technology and following production specifications are all skills that are becoming increasingly important.

- Those of you who are forty-five plus will be able to re-train and take up new work opportunities in areas where your expertise and life experience will be highly valued.

- You'll continue working longer, moving into new areas of employment.

- Part-time, short-term and flexible employment will be the norm and you'll have the opportunity to adjust your work patterns to fit in with your families.

In order to be part of this workshift and thrive and survive in the new ways of working you will have to adapt and in some instances make huge life changes and be prepared to alter your mind set, not only in the way that you work but also the work that you do. There are certain keys that will unlock your potential and help you to join the new workshift. The main key factor is that the kick off point for success has to come from you. Here are some valuable key points.

- Look at change as being positive and be prepared to make several career changes, not just job changes.

- Investigate what work is in and what work is out before you retrain or make a career move.

- Stop thinking in terms of a nine-to-five job, continuous employment and a career in one field. Start thinking about flexible ways of working. Mix and match employment – for example there isn't any reason why you can't be an accountant three days a week and a dance teacher the other two.

- If you have more than one employer or are working part time you will have to become more highly organised and be first rate at time keeping and forward planning. Remember, if you have more than one employer you must find a way that works for you of separating each job, what that job entails and what your employers expect from you.

- If you are going to be self-employed, a homeworker or running your own business you will have to have general business skills such as regular invoicing, tax, marketing, pensions, cash flow, employing others, health and safety, secretarial, diary keeping, finding new clients and customers and watching market prices and practices. Local adult education, business colleges and the Shell LiveWIRE scheme (Chapter 13) all run courses which cover these skills or if you know someone who has worked in these areas ask for their advice. On top of these skills you will also need to learn organisational skills as they are a key to success.

- It's your responsibility to keep up to date with what's happening in your area of employment. It will help if you join a relevant trade organisation, club or trade union. You should go to appropriate exhibitions, lectures and demonstrations. What you learn from them will help to keep you one step ahead of the competition. In the fast changing world of technology this is important. They are also good places to network. Having up to the minute information on relevant areas of your employment will put you one step ahead of the competition in an interview situation. Set aside 'catch up' time, time to catch up with relevant reading material or networking. This updating process should be ongoing, not just when you have an interview, meeting or are thinking of changing jobs. Fine tune your networking, in the playground, the launderette, fitness club, don't put limits.

- Try to persuade your employer to send you on re-training

courses: explain the benefits to the business. Take any re-training your employer is offering. Skills are transferable. But, be prepared to fund your own IT course, or take time out for it. Use the new technology to share your work load.

- If you become a learner-returner ignore the age gap between you and other students. Life and work experiences will give you added self-confidence and people skills. Distance learning requires self discipline.

- If you have to take a lower paid job because that's all that's on offer use it as a way of getting you back onto the employment circuit.

- Include your partner in all plans of flexible working, you may both decide it fits in with your other commitments. The up side of flexible working or role reversal is that it often makes family caring easier and cheaper, creates solid bonds between children and parents and gives retraining time. In a role re-versal relationship make sure that you continue to consider each other as equals. Mutual respect was never more impor-tant in relationships than it is now.

- Don't look at stress as something that happens to somebody else. The Samaritans and similar help organisations (Chapter 13) aren't just there for when you're feeling suicidal.

- Tailor your CV to fit a certain job application. Get the name and job title of the person in the organisation who is in the position to make the hiring decisions. That's the person you target. Research jobs before applying, i.e. send for job descrip-tions, information on organisation, research in library, newspapers, trade directories and on the high street. Scan recruitment ads and articles in business pages for information about new factories or offices or winning new orders or enter-ing new markets. These are clues that the organisation will be hiring additional staff. At an interview show enthusiasm, motivation, leadership, commitment, communication and initiative.

- Practise people skills, use friends and colleagues for rehearsals.

Involve friends, partners, relatives and colleagues with your self skills audit.

- Accept that retirement will probably have to go on the back-burner, look instead at career moves that match your age range.

- Look for the hidden job opportunities. For example, if you want to be a garden designer but it's an overcrowded area investigate the spin offs – garden maintenance, teaching/ writing about horticulture, working in a garden centre or for a garden supplier.

- Practise being assertive in simple ways – start by trying not to panic at the supermarket check-out or being authoritative when you have to return items to shops or make a complaint in restaurants. It all helps to build your positive voice and attitude.

- And last, but not least, hang onto your sense of humour – it's more permanent than your job.

These keys will help you to unlock your skills and talents. You may even find others: add them to the list as reminders.

One of the aims of this book has been to take the fear out of the future by giving you factual information, case histories and practical advice. I believe that we only suffer from fear and anxiety in employment when we feel that we have no control over our situation and no knowledge on which to plan our next move. With this book as your guide you can plan your career changes, free yourself up to be part of a more flexible work force, check that your skills match the job opportunities in the millennium, discover and unlock your true potential and match it to what is available in the job market of the future. This isn't the end of employment, it's the beginning of an employment challenge which you are now ready to take on board successfully.

CHAPTER 12

Jargon

adapters Men who have adapted to women earning more than them.

attachment An addition or 'enclosure' to an e-mail message which can contain computer files, pictures, sound or video.

baby boomers/boomers Those born between 1945 and 1965.

birth dirth Came after boomers.

break-out space Office area where people casually chat.

browsing Jumping from page to page on the World Wide Web.

bullpen Open plan office.

byte A unit of computer data. The way we add up the amount of information stored on a computer hard-drive. Amounts of computer memory are usually measured in kilobytes (kb), megabytes (Mb) or gigabytes (Gb).

career alternate enhancement programme Being downsized.

CD-ROMs Compact discs that contain multimedia computer information – that is pictures, words, speech and music. The ROM stands for 'Read Only Memory'. Each disk can hold vast amounts of information in many different forms. To use a CD-ROM you need a multimedia computer with a CD-ROM drive.

clubbing Where peripatetic workers from many companies, even competing companies, gather every day to work in a space providing private workstations, cafés and meeting rooms, in a club-like environment.

cobweb effect Skills lag behind supplies.

cockpit A small enclosed individual room.

company loyalty A thing of the past, no longer recognised.

competitive Lower prices, highest skills.

convivial carrels Enclosed cubicle spaces for team working.

core re-emphasising Being downsized.

core competencies Attempting to build new business from what a company does best.

data mining The process of sifting through vast amounts of data using neural networks, rule-based systems, case-based reasoning, machine learning and statistical programmes in order to discover new knowledge. This is a new tool for marketeers, financial analysts, scientists, health care professionals and government workers.

decruited Fired.

dehired Fired.

delayering Reduction in the number of management levels and authoritative structures.

delevel Downsized.

dial-up access Connecting to the Internet by dialling in on a telephone account. You have to pay a monthly subscription.

difficult transition To change from pyramid to process.

dinky's A couple who are; Double Income No Kids Yuppies.

desk No longer thought to be needed.

downsizing or rightsizing Delayering the organisation. Flattening the pyramid. Becoming lean and mean.

EDI Electronic data interchange.

empowerment Altering trust, security and informal relationships.

encoding The way a computer translates some e-mail attachments so they can be sent on the Internet.

endangered species Middle Managers.

event, an A meeting.

female jobs Jobs seen to be women orientated, men see them as women's work.

feng shui Means Wind and Water – acupuncture for buildings.

flexible labour market Employability which replaces the traditional employment contract with one that buys temporary loyalty sometimes in return for career-advancing training but always for lower pay.

floating This is what desks now do.

floppy disk Disk for storing information 3½ inches in diameter inside a hard plastic case. It slots into the computer's floppy disk drive to load, unload or transfer information.

gender work jungle Jobs female/male being redefined.

gold collar worker Someone who is adept at creative thinking, and technology fluent. Matters most to the corporate employer and has a salary to match.

groupware A new generation of software that runs on networked computer systems which enables teams to combine forces across geographic boundaries.

hard (disk) drive Computer's built-in electronic filing cabinet for storing information.

hardware The physical parts that make up the computer and any accessories.

homepage Front page of a website.

homepages An individual personal website.

horizontal process This cuts across departments and functions. Opposite of Pyramid.

hot desking Ensures that office resources are used more efficiently, as in twenty-four hour banking and shift work – sharing the space.

hotelling Turning up and booking a space in a building which isn't your own, which has hotel standard service.

individual workplace responsibility Taking responsibility for the individual and even shared spaces they use during the workday.

infomated Manager's jobs that have been automated by IT.

information super highway Buzz words. Information it is, but no one knows where the super comes from.

interactive Information displayed by a computer which you can control or influence, such as answering questions or playing a game on the screen.

Internet Began as a communications system for the US military in the event of a nuclear conflict. It is now an international network of computer networks. Using the Internet you can exchange electronic mail with some 40 million people.

Internet access provider (IAP) Offers you services ranging from dial-up accounts to virtual servers. IAPs are more geared to providing a practical and cost-effective service and are generally the preferred choice of businesses seeking to establish an Internet presence.

Internet service provider (ISP) Usually provides a range of information services in addition to standard dial-up accounts. It is aimed at the individual Internet subscriber. The range of technical services available from ISPs is usually more limited than those available from IAPs.

Intranet A mini-Internet within your own company that allows computers to talk to one another.

involuntarily severed from it Being downsized.

IRC Internet Relay Chat or various interest groups.

jobs not going forward Being downsized.

knowledge workers Professionals, technicians and those who are educated and trained in a particular type of knowledge and applied technology.

lagoon An outward facing group of people working together.

LAN Local Area Networks.

LAN managers These run Intranets.

lap-top A computer with a keyboard and a screen that is compact and portable.

lean manufacturing time-based management Getting it right first time.

learning organisation A company that doesn't forget every-thing it used to know in every succeeding reorganisation.

mailbox An electronic on-screen post-box containing your incoming e-mail messages. It may blink to let you know mail has arrived.

meeting room Furnished with sofas and lamps – very popular.

middle managers Those who traditionally pass information up and down the hierarchy.

modem A small box or plug-in card that lets your PC connect and 'talk' to other computers over a phone line. Modem stands for 'modulate and demodulate'. It performs the task of taking the digital pulses from the computer and transferring them into analogue waveforms suitable for the telephone system.

mouse A small egg-shaped device wired up to the computer. Sliding it about on the desk moves and controls a small pointer (cursor) on the computer screen.

multimedia The combination of various types of media to appeal to as many senses as possible.

newsgroups These are electronic noticeboards allowing people to talk to one another about their interests. There are currently thousands of newsgroups, covering every possible topic, from cars to politics. Access to newsgroups is usually included as part of your Internet account. Newsgroups bring people together from all sorts of backgrounds and cultures. Useful for networking.

Nintendo generation Those born post boomers.

non-renew Being fired.

off-line Using your computer when it's not connected to the Internet.

office Status symbol on the decline.

on-line Being connected, or able to connect your computer to the Internet.

Orchids Couple who have One Recent Child, Heavily In Debt.

outplaced from it Being fired.

outsourcing Reshaping the organisation, everything that isn't the core. Information services, facilities management, human resources, risk management, engineering services are functions that can all be done away from the organisation and hired in from outside providers.

PC Personal computer.
players Those doing the work.
posting Telling your computer to send an e-mail message.
process leaders Name for directors.

quiet room Work area for decision making or private conversation.

RAM (Random Access Memory) Computer memory which stores instructions and information that can be easily accessed and changed.
Rambo school of hiring and firing Use of ruthless hiring and firing methods.
rationalised Downsized.
rationalised out of the company Fired.
re-engineering Breaking down a company into its essential processes. Challenges non-essential functions and departmental routines that are inefficient, redundant and generally of no value.
realigning Downsizing.
redefine Downsizing.
released Fired.
resisters Men who are resisting female entry into the workforce and resisting the gender swap at home.
restructuring Cutting costs by shedding jobs.
robots Unavailable so far to do housework, but have transformed the car industry, and have created almost workerless factories.
ROM (Read Only Memory) Computer memory holds permanent instructions set during manufacture of the hard disk or CD.
romping Talking, gathering and interacting.

scanner Reads print and pictures and inputs them straight into the computer.

search engine A facility on the Internet which lets you search for particular topics.

server In relation to the Internet, a computer which maintains a constant link to the Net.

shrinkage Smaller workforce.

skill mix adjustment Downsizing.

smart card Security device used for clocking in; credit card with chip embedded in it.

software Instructions which tell your computer how to perform a particular type of task.

strategic alliances Companies that form semi-permanent partnerships to combine resources and enhance competencies.

surfing As in, 'surfing the web.' A trendy term for navigating the World Wide Web.

surplussed Downsized.

telecommuting People who work two or three days a week from home. Not to be mistaken for people who take work home after office hours.

terabyte Is a million, million bytes of information.

touchscreen A screen displaying various options or commands which can be selected by lightly touching its surface with your finger.

TQM Total Quality Management.

trolley Replaces desk and is wheeled to wherever you are working that day.

touchdown stations Filing cabinets on wheels.

universal resort locator Website address.

usenet The area of the Internet that carries newsgroups.

value chains Where a company is one link in an extended value chain connecting a number of producers, suppliers, interim users and end users, all of whom add value to the product process.

virtual organisation Dispensing with the organisation and people altogether by delegating everything to the market.

virtual reality A way of using sophisticated computer animation to represent an environment – for example, the company meeting room – and letting you move about in it.

virus A computer user's nightmare. Viruses are programmes that slip into your hard drive via floppy disk or downloaded from the Internet, and perform all sorts of acts such as incapacitating your system or corrupting or deleting all information from your hard drive.

volume rated production Production schedule adjustment.

voice recognition Allows a computer to recognise instructions by voice. Keyboard skills will go out of the window.

wearable office Portable office equipment, such as the mobile phone, the modem and the lap-top.

Web browser Special software which lets you fetch, view and experience information on Web pages.

Web page Each one has a special address to locate it which begins http://www. By copying this address on to your Web browser, you can tell your computer what page to find.

windows Program that uses 'windows' or boxes in individual areas of the computer screen to gain access to different tasks. Designed to make the computer more user friendly.

wireless networks This technology will not need cabling, and will thus transform older buildings which were unsuitable for the raised floors and suspended ceilings of the modern computerised cabled office.

workchurch The corporate headquarters, as much of a symbolic statement as a medieval cathedral.

working poor People with full time jobs who are stuck in poverty.

worktent Temporary or moveable office space.

World Wide Web (WWW) Millions of 'pages' are held on the part of the Internet called the World Wide Web. Web pages don't just contain pictures and words, they can also include speech, music and video clips. All Web pages are available to anyone for the price of a local phone call.

(some of these descriptions have been adapted from, 'T' *Magazine* Internet Glossary, by John Cook and Ian Cox)

CHAPTER 13

Useful Information

The following lists of organisations, contact numbers and basic explanations of information technology are all relevant to your job search or career change.

UK

(NB: All London dialling codes have been changed from 0171 and 0181 to 020 7 and 020 8 respectively.)

Information Society Initiative (ISI), Business Link Help Desk, Tel: 0345 512288 or call the free 'IT for All' Information line on 0800 456 567. E-mail: info@isi-bltv.co.uk. Website: http://www.isi-bltv.co.uk (A comprehensive package of activities to promote the benefits of using information and communications technologies in the UK.)

Age Works, a service of Ecco Employment Agencies. Tel: 020 7371 5411

Forties People. Tel: 020 7329 4044 (London only)

Careers Continued. Tel: 020 7680 0033 (London only)

Recruit. Tel: 01442 233 550

Age Concern Headquarters, Astral House, 1268 London Road, London SW16 4ER. Tel: 020 8765 7200. Fax: 020 8765 7211. Website: http://www.ace.org.uk. Age Concern Information Line, Tel: 0800 009966 between 7 am and 7 pm or write to Age

Concern Information Line, Freepost SW30375, Ashburton, Devon TW13 7ZZ (Provide factsheets on a wide range of issues for older people.)

Age Resource, c/o Age Concern. Tel: 020 8765 7610. Fax: 020 8679 6069. E-mail: agres@ace.org.uk (For people aged fifty plus.)

The University of the Third Age Headquarters, 26 Harrison Street, London WC1H 8JG. Tel: 020 7837 8838. Fax: 020 7837 8845. E-mail: national.office@u3a.aol.com. Website: http://www.u3a.org.uk (Contact the headquarters to obtain details of your local branch.)

The Open University Headquarters, Walton Hall, Milton Keynes MK7 6AA. Write to Central Enquiry Service, The Open University, PO Box 200, MK7 6YZ. Tel: 01908 653231. Fax: 01908 654806. E-mail: ces-gen@open.ac.uk. Website: http://www.open.ac.uk (Provides distance learning in a wide range of university and college courses.)

The National Extension College, 18 Brooklands Avenue, Cambridge CB2 2HN. Tel: 01223 450200. E-mail: nec@dial.pipex.com. Website: http://www.nec.ac.uk. (Provides distance learning for all areas of education and training.)

UCAS (Universities and Colleges Admissions Service), Rosehill, New Barn Lane, Cheltenham, Gloucestershire GL52 3LZ. Tel: 01242 222444. E-mail: enq@ucas.ac.uk. Website: http://www.ucas.ac.uk. (Application advice for university and college based courses in the UK. Copies of the UCAS Handbook can be found in your local careers service library.)

TECs (Training and Enterprise Councils) operate throughout the UK. Website: http://www.tec.co.uk (Offer business information, advice and counselling and a wide variety of courses in business skills and help for companies wanting to train young people.)

CRAC (Careers Research and Advisory Centre), Sheraton House, Castle Park, Cambridge CB3 0AX. Tel: 01223 460277. Fax: 01223 311708. E-mail: enquiries@CRAC.org.uk. Website: http://www.CRAC.org.uk. (Career development programmes, graduate recruitment and development, training and education. They produce a directory of further and higher education courses in the UK.)

COIC (Careers and Occupational Information Centre), PO Box 298a, Thames Ditton KT7 0ZS. Tel: 020 8957 5030. Fax: 020 8957 5019 (For information on training or returning to education.)

The Universities Association for Continuing Education, University of Leeds, Department of Continuing Education, Leeds LS2 9JT. Tel: 0113 233 4541

The Prince's Youth Business Trust with the Bank of Scotland, call the Royal Bank of Scotland. Tel: 0131 556 855 (Produce a Finance Pack outlining the basic requirements of running business finance, a knowledge of book keeping, taxation and accounts.)

GAP, Gap House, 44 Queens Road, Reading, Berkshire RG1 4BB Tel: 0118 959 4914. Fax: 0118 957 6634. E-mail: volunteer@gap.org.uk. Website: http://www.gap.org.uk (Organise international projects for youth exchange for young people who want to go on an overseas placement, experience a different way of life and work for the benefit of others, in the year between school and going on to higher education at college or university.)

Association of Commonwealth Universities, John Foster House, 36 Gordon Square, London WC1H 0PF. Tel: 020 7387 857. Fax: 020 7387 2655. E-mail: pubinfon@acu.ac.uk. Website: http://www.acu.ac.uk (Publishes the *British Universities Guide to Graduate Study*, which gives details of postgraduate courses lasting a minimum of nine months in UK universities.)

London and South East Regional Advisory Council for Education and Training publishes *A Compendium of Advanced Courses in Colleges of Further and Higher Education*, with details of advanced full-time courses and sandwich courses offered at colleges outside the university sector in England and Wales

The Association of Graduate Careers Advisory Services publishes *Current Vacancies,* a fortnightly listing of job vacancies, and *What Do Graduates do?*, which explains what graduates go on to do after leaving university and which degrees tend to lead to which jobs. It gives information on the graduate job scene, with summaries of the type of work and postgraduate courses entered by students shortly after graduation

University of London Careers Service publish a weekly magazine and vacancy bulletin, *Job Opportunities Bulletin*
'T' training, education employment, Magazine, Highburrow Lane, Wilson Way, Pool, Redruth, Cornwall TR1 2BR. Tel: 01209 313 556
Department for Education and Employment publish *Just The Job*
TUC (Trades Union Congress), Congress House, Great Russell Street, London WC1B 3LS. Tel: 020 7636 4030. Fax: 020 7636 0632. Website: http://www.tuc.org.uk (Deal with employment related issues and education/training for union members.)
The Equal Opportunities Commission, Overseas House, Quay Street, Manchester M3 3HN. Tel: 0161 833 9244. Fax: 0161 835 1657. E-mail: info@eoc.org.uk. Website: http://www.eoc.org.uk (Contact this organisation if you think you are a victim of unfair dismissal, sexual discrimination, pay inequality or harassment in employment.)
The Maternity Alliance, 45 Beech Street, London EC2P 2LX. Tel: 020 7588 8582. Fax: 020 7588 8584. E-mail: ma@mail.pro-net.co.uk (Health and social policy issues in the area of maternity care. *Going Back: A Woman's Guide to Returning to Work After Maternity Leave*, is available from them.)
Parents at Work, 45 Beech Street, Barbican, London EC2P 2LX. Tel: 020 7628 3565
Women Returners Network, 100 Park Village East, London NW1 3SR. Tel: 020 7628 2290/1/2. Fax: 020 7380 0123
The Federation of Small Businesses, 2 Catherine Place, Westminster, London SW1E 6HF. Tel: 020 7233 7900. Website: http://www.fsb.co.uk
Shell LiveWire Hotline Tel: 0345 573 252 (Anybody between the ages of sixteen and thirty who wants advice on starting their own business can contact them for the cost of a local call.)
Telecottage Association, Freepost CV 2312, WREN Telecottage, Kenilworth CV8 2RR. Tel: 01203 696538
National Association of Teleworkers, The Island House, Midsomer Norton, Bath, Avon BA3 2HL. Tel: 01761 413869
New Ways To Work, 309 Upper Street, London N1 2TY. Tel: 020 7226 4026 (They offer their members support and infor-

mation on flexible working arrangements, such as job sharing, term-time working and working from home.)

Home Run, Cribau Mill, Shirenewton, Chepstow NP6 6RD (Offers a free fact sheet on identifying what to do and how to start a home business)

Home Run, 79 Black Lion Lane, London W6 9BG. Tel: 020 8845 9244 (Send an SAE for a fact sheet on starting up a home business.)

British Telecom, Tel: 0800 800 800. Website: http://www. BT.com (Have an assortment of leaflets on teleworking, working from home and flexible working.)

Alternatives in Work, St James's Church, 197 Piccadilly, London W1 0LL. Tel: 020 7781 921 (Run by Nick Williams who gives talks and workshops on alternative ways of running your life, focusing your energy and reprioritising.)

The Data Protection Register, Office of the Data Protection register, Whycliffe House, Water Lane, Wilmslow, Cheshire SK9 5AF. Tel: 01625 545745. Website: http://www.dpr.gov.uk

For help with assertiveness, depression, stress and life management skills you may decide to contact a psychologist or psychotherapist. To find one who concentrates on your particular difficulties look in your local reference library for *The Directory of Chartered Psychologists* and *The National Register of Psychotherapists*. Both of these are published yearly and list qualified and accredited psychotherapists and psychologists, some of whom will specialise in cognitive behaviour training (CBT), particularly relevant to depression associated with unemployment.

British Association of Psychotherapists, 37a Mapesbury Road, London NW2 4HJ. Tel: 020 8452 9823. Fax: 020 8452 5182

British Psychological Society, St Andrews House, 48 Princess Road East, Leicester LE1 7DR. Tel: 0116 254 9568. Fax: 0116 247 0787. E-mail: bps1@le.ac.uk. Website: http://www.bps.org.uk

The Samaritans (branches throughout the UK). Tel: 0345 90 90 90. E-mail: samaritans@anon.twwells.com Website: http://www.samaritans.org.uk (Provide confidential emotional support by telephone or e-mail, especially if you are feeling depressed or suicidal.)

Association of Stress Therapists, Tel: 01843 291255

British Association for Counselling, 1 Regent Place, Rugby, Warwickshire CV21 2PJ. Tel: 01788 578 328. Fax: 01788 562189. E-mail: bac@bac.co.uk. Website: http://www.counselling.co.uk

Centre for Stress Management, 156 Wetcombe Hill, Blackheath, London SE3 7DH. Tel: 020 8293 4114. Fax: 020 8293 1441. E-mail: centreforstressmanagement@btinternet.com

The Women's Therapy Centre, 10 Manor Gardens, London N7 6JS. Tel: 020 7263 6200. Fax: 020 7281 7879

The British Wheel of Yoga, 1 Hamilton Place, Boston Road, Sleaford, Lincolnshire NG34 7ES. Tel: 01529 306851. Fax: 01529 303233. E-mail: wheelyoga@aol.com. Website: http://www.members.aol.com/wheelyoga

The Positive Health Centre, 101 Harley Street, London W1N 1AF. Tel: 020 7935 1811. (Provides autogenic training, a series of mental exercises that ease the physical symptoms of stress.)

Alexander Technique International, 66C Thurlestone Road, West Norwood, London SE27 0PD. Tel: 020 7880253. E-mail: uk@ati-net.com (This method helps you to become aware of balance and posture at work. Send an SAE for a list of teachers.)

The Institute of Management, Management House, Cottingham Road, Corby, Northants NN17 1TT. Tel: 01536 204222 (One-to-one career counselling interviews. A database of members looking for new posts. A telephone employment helpline for legal problems. One-day seminars covering job-search topics.)

The Management Information Centre, compiles reading lists on a range of subjects from: Redundancy, Career Planning, Redundancy Policies and Payments, Job Hunting, Setting up as a Consultant. Reading lists are provided free to members

The Institute of Personnel and Development, IPD House, Camp Road, London SW19 4UX and 2 Savoy Court WC2. Tel: 020 8971 9000

The Royal Society for the Encouragement of Arts, Manufacturers and Commerce, 8 John Adam Street, London WC2 6EZ (Report, *Redefining Work*, 1998.)

The Joseph Rowntree Foundation, Tel: 01904 629241 (Books and journals.)

DEMOS, 9 Bridewell Place, London EC4 6AP. Tel: 020 7353 4479 (An independent think tank, publishes books and journals.)

Overseas Job Express, Premier House, Shoreham Airport, Sussex BN43 5FF (*Overseas Job Express*, a twice-monthly newspaper sold by subscription.)

Employment Services, Overseas Placement Unit, c/o Rockingham House, 123 West Street, Sheffield S1 4ER. Tel: 0114 259 6051 (The Overseas Placement Unit (OPU) of the Employment Service offers advice and guidance to people who want to work overseas and has a limited range of overseas vacancies. To apply for these vacancies you should ask at your local Job Centre for information on the OPU. They also have a range of country fact sheets giving advice on working abroad.)

VSO (Voluntary Services Overseas), 317 Putney Bridge Road, Putney, London SW15 2PN. Tel: 020 8780 2266. Website: http://www.vso.org.uk (For skilled people who want to work overseas, generally in third world countries.)

Common Purpose, 55 City Road, London EC1. Tel: 020 7608 8100

USA

AARP (American Association of Retired Persons), 601 E St. New, Washington, DC 20049. Tel: (800) 424 3410. Website: http://www.aarp.org/working-options (Non-profit organisation dedicated to helping older Americans, offering advice on a wide range of things including careers.)

Senior Net, 121 Second Street, 7th Floor, San Francisco, CA 94105. Fax: (415) 495 3999 (Offers low-cost introductions to basic computer skills.)

The Open University of the United States is currently seeking accreditation but hopes to open soon offering the same facilities as its UK counterpart. E-mail: open-university-USA@ open.ac.uk. Website: http://www.open.edu

Elderhostel Institute Network, 75 Federal Street, Boston, MA

02110. E-mail: network@elderhostel.org (A network throughout the US, Canada and Bermuda which is the umbrella
organisation for Learning in Retirement (LIR), offering education for those who are fifty plus.)

The US Equal Employment Opportunity Commission. Tel:
(800) 669 4000. Website: http://www.eeoc.gov

The Whirlpool Foundation, A Study of Western European
Women's Views on Work, Family & Society, 400 Riverview
Drive, Suite 410, Benton Harbour, MI 49022

New Ways To Work, 785 Market Street, Suite 950, San
Francisco, California 94103. Tel: (415) 995 9860

The Homeworkers Union and Small Business Association, 380
Lexington Avenue, Suite 1700, New York 10168. Tel: (212) 599
4345. Fax: (212) 599 4346. E-mail: help@telecommuting-
jobs.org. Website: http://www.telecommuting-jobs.org

The United States Federation of Small Businesses, Tel: (800)
637 3331 between 9 am and 5 pm. Website:
http://www.usfsb.com

American Small Business Assocation, Tel: (800) 8-ASK-SBA

Alexander Technique International, 1692 Massachusetts
Avenue, 3rd Floor, Cambridge, MA 02138. Toll free: (888) 321
0856. Tel: (617) 497 2242. Fax: (617) 497 2615. E-mail:
usa@ati-net.com

The World Bank, 1818 H Street NW, Washington DC, 20433.
Tel: 01420-868480 for World Bank Foundations (Publishes
books and journals.)

Homefair, for relocating information across the US. Gives
regional salary differences, information on local schools, home
finding, helps you to pick your own list of the ten best cities to
live in. http.//homefair.com/hom

AUSTRALIA AND NEW ZEALAND

Age Concern New Zealand Inc, 3rd Floor, Riddiford House, 150
Featherston Street, Wellington, New Zealand. Write to Age
Concern New Zealand, PO Box 10 688, Wellington, New
Zealand. Tel: (04) 471 2709. Fax: (04) 473 2504. E-mail:

national.office@ageconcern.org.nz.   Website: http://www.
ageconcer.org.nz
Age Concern (Otago), PO Box 5355, Dunedin, New Zealand.
Tel: (03) 477 1040. Fax: (03) 477 1040 during office hours.
Website: http://www.earthlight.co.nz/~agecon
Human Rights and Equal Opportunities Commission, Central
Office, Level 8, Piccadilly Tower, 133 Castlereagh Street,
Sydney, NSW 2000, Australia. GPO Box 5218, Sydney NSW
1042. Tel: (02) 9284 9609. Fax: (02) 9284 9611. Website:
http://www.hreoc.gov.au
Equal Opportunities Employment Commission, 4th Floor,
Southpac Tower, Corner Queen and Custom Streets, PO Box
6751, Wellesley Street, Auckland, New Zealand. Tel: (64) 9309
0874
Office of Women's Affairs, Level 18, Mineral House, 41 George
Street, Brisbane, Queensland 4000, Australia. Write to: PO Box
390, Albert Street, Brisbane, Queensland 4002, Australia. Tel:
(07) 3224 4062. E-mail: infolink@treasury.qld.gov.au
Maternity Alliance, PO Box 86, Asquith, NSW 2077, Australia.
Tel: (049) 61 1626. Fax: (049) 61 3404. E-mail:
mavoice@ozemail.com.au.   Website: http://www.ozemail.
com.au/~mavoice
Australian Small Business Association, 213 Greenhill Road,
Eastwood, South Australia 5063. Write to: GPO Box 2315,
Adelaide, South Australia 5001. Free call: (1800) 808 463. Fax:
(08) 223 2500. E-mail: asba@essential.com.au. Website:
http://www.cpsu.asn.au/~asba
Alexander Technique International, 11/11 Stanley Street,
Darlinghurst, NSW 2010, Australia. Tel: (02) 331 7563. E-
mail: australia@ati-net.com
New Zealand Council of Trade Unions, PO Box 6645
Wellington, Tel: (04) 385 1334. E-mail: ctu@hq.nzctu.union.
org.nz
Australian Council of Trade Unions, North Wing, Trades Hall,
54 Victoria Street, Victoria 3053. Tel: (03) 9663 5266. E-mail:
mailbox@actu.asn.au
The Australian Institute of Management, AIM National Office,
Management House, 181 Fitzroy Street, St Kilda, Victoria 3182.

Write to AIM National Office, PO Box 112, St Kilda, Victoria
3182. Tel: (03) 9534 818. E-mail: national@aim.can.au
The **U3A** offering education and learning for those who are fifty
plus have groups throughout Australia. E-mail: www.
u3acanberra.org.au

DIRECTORIES

UK

Directory of Jobs and Careers Abroad by Alex Lipinski, published
by Vacation Work. (Looks at a range of job options abroad
from two weeks in France to two-year contracts in the Middle
East to permanent emigration to New Zealand.)
Kompas   Basic corporate data on over 400 leading companies in
British industry
Dun & Bradstreet Key British Enterprises   Basic corporate data
on Britain's top 50,000 companies
Kelly's Business Directory   Information on UK-based companies
Who Owns Whom   Parent companies, subsidiaries and associates
Hambro Corporate Register   Vital corporate and financial facts
on all UK quoted companies
Directory of Directors   Lists 60,000 directors of British compa-
nies and their directorships
Stock Exchange Year Book   Gives a brief financial description of
all quoted public companies
*Britain's Top 2000 Private Companies/Britain's Second 2000 Private
Companies* (from Jordan Information Services)   Two directo-
ries of major British companies, providing trading and financial
information
Registrar of Companies and Limited Partnerships, Companies
House, Crown Way, Maindy, Cardiff CF4 3UZ. Tel: 01222 388
588
Register of Companies   Latest accounts, balance sheets, names of
directors and other financial information
Companies House, 55–71 City Road, London EC1Y 1BB. Tel: 020
7253 9393 (A search fee is payable.)

To find the recruitment agencies and consultancies that are right for you look in:

The *Yellow Pages* or *Thomsons* directory

The Directory of Trainer Support Services (published by Kogan Page)

The Yearbook of Recruitment and Employment Services (Federation of Recruitment and Employment Services)

Hoover's Handbook of World Business Everything you need to know about the most important European companies and countries.

USA

Hoover's Handbook of American Business Profiles of over 500 major America companies.

DATABASES

UK

Infocheck Check rating and financial data on over 420,000 UK limited companies

Jordan's Full company accounts for 100,000 UK limited companies

Kompass UK Corporate and financial data on 150,000 UK companies

Reuters Textline Up-to-date articles on companies from the UK and international press

Dun & Bradstreet Financial data on turnover and capital, details of trade, trade names, trading styles and a full list of directors by name and job description

INTERNET

The following companies provide access to the Internet:
CompuServe, Tel: 0990 000400. Fax: 0117 925 2210

AOL (America OnLine) Tel: 0800 376 5436 (The biggest Internet Service Provider in the world.)
Demon Internet Ltd, Tel: 020 8371 1000. Fax: 020 8371 1150

To date there are around 6,500 Internet Service Providers world wide and the number is growing. The future is probably with free ISPs who make their profit not directly from the user but by either advertising, taking a percentage of the telephone companies', profits or expensive help lines.

For further information on Internet Service Providers world wide contact: http://www.internet.com

To find anything on the Internet you have to use a search engine, there are many to choose from, but the largest are: Yahoo, Alta Vista, HotBot, Lycos or Excite. These are available worldwide.

Index

THE CONFIDENCE TO BE YOURSELF
How to boost your self-esteem
Brian Roet
ISBN 0-7499-1926-4
£8.99 pbk

TOTAL CONFIDENCE
The complete guide to self-assurance and personal success
Philippa Davies
ISBN 0-7499-1434-3
£9.99 pbk

YOUR TOTAL IMAGE
How to communicate success
Philippa Davies
ISBN 0-7499-1641-9
£9.99 pbk

LIFE COACHING
Change your life in 7 Days
Eileen Mulligan
ISBN 0-7499-1937-X
£8.99 pbk

CONFIDENT PUBLIC SPEAKING
How to communicate effectively using the PowerTalk system
Christian H. Godefroy & Stephanie Barrat
ISBN 0-7499-1827-6
£9.99 pbk

SAY WHAT YOU MEAN AND GET WHAT YOU WANT
How to speak the language of success
George R. Walther
ISBN 0-7499-1203-0
£8.99 pbk

Forthcoming titles

MANAGE YOURSELF, MANAGE YOUR LIFE
Vital NLP techniques for personal well-being and professional success
Ian McDermott & Ian Shircore
ISBN 0-7499-1990-6
£9.99 pbk
September 1999

CAROL SPENSER'S STYLE DIRECTIONS FOR WOMEN
Carol Spenser
ISBN 0-7499-1955-8
£17.99 hbk
October 1999

CAROL SPENSER'S STYLE DIRECTIONS FOR MEN
Carol Spenser
ISBN 0-7499-1865-9
£17.99 hbk
October 1999